# Quiet Moments Alone With God

# Emilie Barnes

HARVEST HOUSE PUBLISHERS

EUGENE, OREGON

*Cover by Dugan Design Group, Bloomington, Minnesota*

*Cover illustration © iStockphoto*

Material taken from *15 Minutes Alone with God* and *15 Minutes of Peace with God.*

**QUIET MOMENTS ALONE WITH GOD**
Copyright © 1994/1997 by Emilie Barnes
Published by Harvest House Publishers
Eugene, Oregon 97402
www.harvesthousepublishers.com

Library of Congress Cataloging-in-Publication Data
Barnes, Emilie.
　[15 minutes alone with God]
　Quiet moments alone with God / Emilie Barnes.
　　p. cm.
　ISBN 978-0-7369-2256-2 (pbk.)
　1. Christian women—Prayers and devotions.  I. Barnes, Emilie. 15 minutes
of peace with God. II. Title.
　BV4844.B35 2008
　242'.643—dc20

　　　　　　　　　　　　　　　　　　　　　　　　　　2008031426

**Printed in China**

10 11 12 13 14 15 16 / RDS-SK / 12 11 10 9 8 7 6 5

*This book is dedicated to my very dear friend, Donna Otto of Scottsdale, Arizona. She is my mentor and encourager—teaching me how to have a consistent quiet time with my Lord. Because of her example and helpful suggestions, I now have my very own "prayer closet." When I go there, I am reminded of her inspiration.*

*Thank you, Donna, for your encouragement—for helping me to grow stronger spiritually and to know better my Savior Jesus.*

*–Emilie–*

# A Quiet Moment with Emilie

The idea of having a quiet moment every day draws me in. I so long for these special times...when I can escape from this fast-paced journey called *life*.

The thoughts found on the following pages will give you a good excuse to separate yourself from the busy world and be alone with God—just the two of you. As the psalmist encourages us to "be still and know that [He is] God," I pray that each devotion may challenge you to move closer to Him. Let the words inspire you to take action in your life, become a doer of God's Word, and experience the peace God brings to your stillness.

May you learn to cherish the quiet moments and trust and obey Jesus in every part of your life.

–Emilie

# Becoming New, Becoming Strong

**Scripture Reading:** 2 Corinthians 5:15-18
**Key Verse:** 2 Corinthians 5:17

*Therefore, if anyone is in Christ, he is a new creation; the old has gone, the new has come!*

Becoming a woman of God begins with making a personal commitment to Jesus Christ. Only He can give us the strength to change. Only He can give us the fresh start that allows the spirit of godliness to grow strong in us.

Second Corinthians 5:17 reminds us, "If anyone is in Christ, he is a new creation; the old has gone, the new has come!" That's what I discovered many years ago when I, a 16-year-old Jewish girl, received Christ into my heart. My life began to change from that moment on, and the years since then have been an exciting adventure.

It hasn't always been easy. I've had to give up much bitterness, anger, fear, hatred, and resentment. Many times I've had to back up and start over, asking God to take control of my life and show me His way to live. But as I learned to follow Him, God has guided me through times of pain and joy, struggle and growth. And how rewarding it has been to see the spirit of godliness take root and grow in my life! I give thanks and praise for all His goodness to me over the years.

I'm not finished yet—far from it. Growing in godliness is a lifelong process. And although God is the one who makes it possible, He requires my cooperation. If I want the spirit of godliness to shine in my life and in my home, I must be willing to change what God wants me to change and learn what He wants to teach me. How? Here are some of the ways I've learned to keep myself open to the spirit of godliness.

God's Word is the foundation of my security and strength. Only through daily prayer and meditation can I tap into God's strength and love and get a handle on what He wants for my life.

Because I sometimes need a nudge to keep these disciplines regular and meaningful, I have gotten in the habit of keeping a prayer basket close at hand. This pretty little carryall (I like to use a soft, heart-shaped basket in pastel colors) keeps in one place the tools I need to keep in regular touch with God. My prayer basket contains:

- A *Bible* to prepare my mind and heart to communicate with God
- A *daily devotional* or other inspirational reading

- My *prayer notebook* (more on this later)

- A *bunch of silk flowers* to remind me of the beauty and fragrance of the Lord Jesus Himself

- A *small box of tissues* for the days I cry in joy or pain

- A *pen* for journaling my prayers and writing notes

- A few *pretty postcards or notes* for when I feel moved to communicate God's love to someone I'm praying for

Seeing my basket waiting for me is a wonderful invitation to times of prayer, and a reminder when I haven't taken the time to pray. And it is so convenient to pick up and take to my prayer closet for a quiet time of communion with my heavenly Father.

Where is my closet? It may be a different place every day. (That's the beauty of the portable prayer basket.) Sometimes I settle down at my desk for a quiet time with God. Other times I use the bed, the breakfast room table, the bathtub, a chair by the fireplace, the front yard by the pond, or under a tree—anywhere where I can enjoy privacy.

The actual content of my devotional times varies according to how much time I have available. But generally I start by reading a brief inspirational message from a book. And then I pray. Next I open my Bible and read a chapter or more. (If time is really short, it may be only a verse.)

Next, I turn to my prayer notebook. This is a tool I developed many years ago to help me remember prayer requests and pray more effectively for others. My prayer notebook is a simple 8½ x 11-inch loose-leaf notebook divided into seven sections—one for each day of the week. I've divided all the people and projects I want to pray for—family, friends, church, finances, and so on—into the various sections. For instance, I reserve Mondays to pray for my family, Tuesdays for my church and its servants and activities, Wednesdays for my personal concerns, and so on. (I reserve Sunday for sermon notes and outlines.) Organizing my prayer times in this way keeps me from being overwhelmed while reminding me to be faithful in my prayer life.

I have filled my prayer notebook with photos of people I'm praying for, information about their interests and needs, and special things to remember about them. When I receive prayer requests, I assign them a place in my prayer notebook. I also go through my notebook from time to time and weed out old requests so I don't become overwhelmed. This little book has become a creative, colorful companion that is so close to my heart.

In the back of my prayer notebook, I keep a supply of blank paper for journaling my prayers. This has not been an easy habit for me to develop. I do so much writing for magazine articles, books, letters, and such that writing feels like more work. But for the past few years I have made the effort to write down my praises, my confessions, my thanks, and my requests. I give the Lord my hurts, my pain from the past, my disappointments, and all the questions my mind can think of—in writing. I also write down the convictions of what I hear God saying to me. I'm learning firsthand the benefits of putting my conversations with God in written form:

- *I am able to verbalize things I've held in my heart but never spoken about.* The act of writing somehow seems to bring up my thoughts, feelings, and desires and to expose them to the light of God's love.

- *Writing out my confessions helps me get honest with the Lord.* Somehow a confession feels more real when it's down there in black and white. But this means that God's forgiveness feels more real, too.

- *I can see concrete evidence of my spiritual life*—and my spiritual growth—when I read back over past prayers.

- *My faith grows as I see God's answers more clearly*— God's "yeses," "nos," and "waits." Writing down the answers I think I hear helps me to discern which ones really are of God.

- *My obedience is strengthened.* Once again, written promises are harder to ignore than mental ones. Once I have written down my sense of what God wants me to do, I am more likely to follow through.

There is another kind of writing that I often do during my prayer times. Often while I am praying, God will bring to mind someone who needs my love or care. That's what the note cards are for. When God brings someone to mind, I try to stop right there and drop that person a line, assuring him or her of God's love and my prayers. Having the materials right there at hand makes this encouraging habit easy to maintain. It takes 21 days to form a habit. Start today.

*Father God, instill in me the desire to commune with You each day in prayer. My days are busy and I often can't get done what I already need to do, but, God, I beg You to touch my life in a marvelous way so I can find time to be with You. Please be near to me and bless me when I'm in Your presence. Amen.*

# Stand by Your God

**Scripture Reading:** Psalm 116:1-2
**Key Verse:** Psalm 116:2b

*I will call on him as long as I live.*

*C*onsider the fruit that comes from spending time with your heavenly Father. In Galatians 5, Paul writes that "the fruit of the Spirit is love, joy, peace, patience, kindness, goodness, faithfulness, gentleness, self-control" (verses 22-23). Think about each item in that list. Which of us doesn't need a touch of God's love, patience, kindness, goodness, gentleness, and self-control in our life? Those are the things—as well as guidance, wisdom, hope, and a deeper knowledge of Him—that He wants to give to us as His children.

"But," you say, "who has time? My 'To Do' list is always longer than my day. I run from the time the alarm goes off in the morning until I fall into bed at night. How can I possibly find time to do one more thing? When could I find even a few minutes to read the Bible or pray?"

I answer your questions with a question: Are you

doing what's *important* in your day—or only what is *urgent?*

People do what they want to do. All of us make choices, and when we don't make time for God in our day, when we don't make time for the most important relationship in our life, we are probably not making the best choices.

God greatly desires to spend time alone with you. After all, you are His child (John 1:12; Galatians 3:26). He created you, He loves you, and He gave His only Son for your salvation. Your heavenly Father wants to know you, and He wants you to know Him. The Creator of the universe wants to meet with you alone daily. How can you say no to such an opportunity?

So make it your priority to spend time with God daily. There's not a single right time or one correct place. The only requirement for a right time with God is your willing heart. Your meeting time with God will vary according to the season of your life and the schedules you are juggling. Jesus often slipped away to be alone in prayer (Luke 5:16), but even His prayer times varied. He prayed in the morning and late at night, on a hill and in the upper room (Matthew 14:23; Mark 1:35; Luke 22:41-45; John 17).

I know people who spend hours commuting on the California freeways who use that time to be with God. I used to get up earlier than the rest of the family for a quiet time of reading the Scripture and praying. Now that the children are raised and the home is quiet, I find morning is still best for me, before the telephone starts to ring or I get involved in the day's schedule. And maybe I'm one of the oddballs, but I love getting to church early and having 10 or 15 minutes to open my Bible and think upon God's thoughts. Despite the distracting talk that is often going on around me, I use this block of time to prepare my heart for worship. (In fact, I believe if more members of the congregation devoted time to reading Scripture and praying for the service before the service, church would be more meaningful for every worshiper.)

Again, the times and places where we meet God will vary, but the fact that we meet alone with God each day should be a constant in our life. After all, God has made it clear that He is interested in us who are His children (1 Peter 5:7).

What should you do in your time alone with God? After you've read and meditated on God's Word for a while, spend some time with Him in prayer. Talk to Him as you would to your earthly parent or a special friend who loves you, desires the best for you, and wants to help you in every way possible.

Are you wondering what to talk to God about when you pray? Here are a few suggestions:

- *Praise* God for who He is, the Creator and Sustainer of the whole universe who is interested in each of us who are in His family (Psalm 150; Matthew 10:30).

- *Thank* God for all He has done for you…for all He is doing for you…and for all that He will do for you in the future (Philippians 4:6).

- *Confess* your sins. Tell God about the things you have done and said and thought for which you are sorry. He tells us in 1 John 1:9 that He is "faithful and righteous to forgive us our sins."

- *Pray* for your family…and for friends or neighbors who have needs, physical or spiritual. Ask God to work in the heart of someone you hope will come to know Jesus as Savior. Pray for our government officials, for your minister and church officers, for missionaries and other Christian servants (Philippians 2:4).

- *Pray,* too, for yourself. Ask for guidance for the day ahead. Ask God to help you do His will… and ask Him to arrange opportunities to serve Him throughout the day (Philippians 4:6).

Time with your heavenly Father is never wasted. If you spend time alone with God in the morning, you'll start your day refreshed and ready for whatever comes your way. If you spend time alone with Him in the evening, you'll go to sleep relaxed, resting in His care and ready for a new day to serve Him.

Remember, too, that you can talk to Him anytime, anywhere—in school, at work, on the freeway, at home—about anything. You don't have to make an appointment to ask Him for something you need or to thank Him for something you have received from Him. God is interested in everything that happens to you.

*Father God, may I never forget to call on You in every situation. I want to call on You every day of my life and bring before You my adoration, confession, thanksgiving, and supplication. Thank You for being within the sound of my voice and only a thought's distance away. Amen.*

# Do You Love Me?

**Scripture Reading:** John 21:15-22

**Key Verse:** John 21:15a (NASB)

*Jesus said to Simon Peter, "Simon, son of John, do you love Me more than these?"*

It seems as though we go through life wondering if our husbands, our children, and our friends love us. We feel insecure about the other people in our lives, and we're not sure where we stand. Even though we tell and show everyone we love them, they don't seem to catch the answer, because they're always reaching out to test our love for them.

Sometimes our children wear crazy clothes, put rings in their ears, color their hair in strange colors, and use foul language to see if we really love them. Our whole culture is continually testing us to see if we really love them.

In our passage today Jesus asks Peter three times (after His crucifixion and resurrection and Peter's recent denial of Him) whether Peter really loves Him.

I believe that these basic questions…

- Do you love Me? (verse 15)
- Do you love Me? (verse 16)
- Do you love Me? (verse 17)…

correspond to Peter's three denials of Jesus (John 13:38). Jesus in all His love for Peter wanted to give him a second chance to follow Him. He didn't want Peter to go all through life with the stigma of denying Jesus before His crucifixion. He wanted Peter to know that he was forgiven for his wrongdoings and that he could have a valuable ministry in spreading the gospel throughout the world.

But before Peter was able to confirm his love for Jesus, Jesus stated in verses 18 and 19 that the decision was going to cost him a price. In fact Peter and his wife were crucified upside down approximately 40 years later. After stating that there would be a price for following Him Jesus said, "Follow me," and Peter did.

In repentance and rest is your salvation, in quietness and trust is your strength.

–Isaiah 30:15

Yes, love has its price, not always to the extreme of Peter's, but a price of time, energy, commitment, money, and devotion. Selfish people take without giving back, but a true lover of people is always giving and giving and giving.

Is there someone in your life who is asking the very basic question "Do you love me?" What is your reply?

*Father God, I know there are times when You ask me, "Do you love Me?" I want to answer yes, and, like Peter, I want to follow You. Give me the courage to put my love into action. We can all answer yes, but it is only when we move into action that true love for You is demonstrated. Amen.*

# To Pray Is to Work—
# To Work Is to Pray

**Scripture Reading:** Proverbs 31:10-31
**Key Verse:** Proverbs 31:31 (NASB)

*Give her the product of her hands, and let
her works praise her in the gates.*

For some reason we think that women going to work started during World War II, when women had to fill the gap while the men were away defending our country. But today's Scripture reading goes back to about 800 years B.C. Long before we even thought of women being in the labor force, this capable woman was an energetic, hard worker who labored far into the night.

We see her virtues by looking at the following verses in Proverbs 31:

- 13: She looks for wool and flax. She works with her hands in delight.

- 14: She is like a merchant ship. She brings her food from afar.

- 15: She rises before sunup. She feeds her house-hold. She gives to her maidens.
- 16: She considers real estate. She has her own money. She plants vineyards.
- 17: She works out and is in good physical shape.
- 18: She analyzes her profits. She plans ahead. She works into the night.
- 19-20: She gives to those in need.
- 21: She sews her household's garments.
- 24: She sews to sell for a profit.
- 25-27: She radiates good business practices.
- 28-29: She attracts compliments from her family.
- 31: She exudes excellence from her work and is praised in her neighborhood.

This woman knew all about work even though she didn't have an MBA from Harvard or Stanford. She was a woman who feared (respected) God, and because of her noble efforts in the workplace she was praised.

In today's work climate we find that Monday is the most difficult day of the week—the most absenteeism, the most accidents, the most illnesses. Many of today's workers focus on Fridays—the getaway days. In fact, a popular restaurant is named T.G.I. Friday's (Thank Goodness It's Friday). If you go into this restaurant to eat, you sense a party atmosphere. It's a place to forget all your cares. Let's have a party!

This attitude has a lot to say about modern man's approach to work. It's a far cry from the day when the adage was "To pray is to work, to work is to pray." In those days work was a reflection of worship to God. When we worked we worked to the Lord, not the pleasing of man. That's when the artisan was a creator of excellence in art, music, literature, and the professions. Martin Luther once said that a man can milk cows to the glory of God. It is our own attitude toward work that reflects the joy of the Lord.

Oh, if we could recapture this concept of work! We would take the drudgeries of everyday life and give them to God. If we took the routines surrounding our work and began to pray about them, I believe our whole attitude would change for ourselves and those in our family. No longer would we wait for the whistle to blow on Friday so we could let the real life begin. For us every day would be a Friday.

In Genesis we read that in the beginning God *created*. He believed in the honor of work. It was a godly activity. It was not cursed, as it is today. God worked for six days and then rested. How is your rest period? Do you get any?

Jesus, a carpenter, was a worker making goods out of wood. The Scriptures teach that if we aren't willing to work, we shouldn't expect to eat.

How do we learn that to pray is to work, and to work is to pray?

- Each morning when we wake up, we thank God for a new day and all that is in it.

- We offer to God in worship all of our energies, creativity, time, and skills.

- We recognize that work done in an attitude of prayer brings excellence, which in turn bears testimony to God.

- We realize that we are obedient to God when we provide for our family and their needs.

- We model to our children that work is good, so that they see us give worship to God for the work He has given us.

*Father God, at times when I face the drudgeries of all that I have to do, when I wipe the sweat from my brow and my back aches from the weight of lifting, I forget that how I do my job is a reflection upon my worship to You. I truly want to wake up each morning with a song in my heart and an eagerness to start a new day. In the evening before I fall asleep I want to praise You for another day's work. Let me be in continuous prayer while at work. Let me work for You and forget about the praises of man. Amen.*

# God Has a Master Plan

**Scripture Reading:** Jeremiah 18:2-6
**Key Verse:** Jeremiah 18:6

*O house of Israel, can I not do with you as this potter does?*

When our son Brad was in elementary school one of his class projects was to shape clay into something. Brad made a reddish dinosaur-type thing. It's on my bookshelf today as a display of Brad's first work of art—molded and shaped with his small hands, brought home to me with pride.

In high school Brad enrolled in a ceramics class as one of his electives. His first pieces were crooked and misshapen, but as time went on he was able to fashion beautiful works of art. He made vases, pots, pitchers, a butter pot, and many other kinds of pottery. Many pieces of clay were thrown on the wheel to become beautiful, but during the process they would take a different direction. Brad would then work and work to reshape them, and sometimes he would have to start all over, working

27

and working again to make each piece just as he wanted it to be.

God has taken, so to speak, a handful of clay in each one of us. He is the Master Potter. We are the vessels in His house. Each one He knows intimately. Each one is different.

We might ask ourselves, "What kind of vessel am I?" Maybe the pot that holds a plant, its roots growing deep in the soil that produces the beauty above in a flowering bloom. Or a cup to hold the tea of friendship. Or a pitcher from which flows the words of wisdom, or a casserole dish with a tightly-sealed lid so nothing from inside will leak out.

Almighty God picks us up like a piece of ugly clay and begins to shape our lives. On the potter's wheel we begin to spin around. God says, "I want you to be strong and beautiful inside and out." The hands of God move up and down as the wheel spins, forming with one hand the inside and with the other the outer side. He says, "I'm with you. I am the Lord of your life, and I will build within you a strong foundation based upon the Word of God."

It feels so good to us as we grow in beauty. Then something happens in our life—a child dies, fire takes our home, we lose our job, our husband leaves, a child rebels. The world cries out to us, "Stop! Jump off the potter's wheel and come with me. I'll give you what you need to feel good." So we place the lid on our vessel and we escape inside ourselves to try to forget the hurt and pain we feel. The beauty God was shaping is put on the shelf only to get dusty and pushed to the back behind all the books and magazines. We feel so lost and far from God as time passes. We've become sidetracked, and yet God has not sidetracked us. He says, "I will never leave you nor forsake you."

I love the bumper sticker I saw, "If you feel far from God, guess who moved?" It wasn't God who placed you on the shelf. *We* are the ones who tighten the lids on our hearts, who put ourselves on the shelf. It's time to push off the lid and jump back on the potter's wheel. We need to become obedient to Almighty God, the Master Potter. He will take the time we were sidetracked and use it to help mold us into His master plan.

In pottery the true beauty of the clay comes out after the firing in the kiln. Allow the Lord to use the negatives in your life to become someone of beauty.

> *Father God, You truly are the potter and I am the clay. Mold me into the person You want me to be, not what I want to be. I know that is placing a lot of trust in You, but I know that You love me and are concerned about me. May my clay pottery reflect Your light like a fine porcelain vessel. Amen.*

# Seek His Thoughts

**Scripture Reading:** Isaiah 55:6-13

**Key Verse:** Isaiah 55:8 (NASB)

*"My thoughts are not your thoughts, neither are*
*your ways My ways," declares the LORD.*

Suppose a man should find a great basket by the wayside, carefully packed, and upon opening it he should find it filled with human thoughts—all the thoughts which had passed through one single brain in one year or five years. What a medley they would make! How many thoughts would be wild and foolish, how many weak and contemptible, how many mean and vile, how many so contradictory and crooked that they could hardly lie still in the basket. And suppose he should be told that these were all his *own* thoughts, children of his own brain; how amazed he would be, and how little prepared to see himself as revealed in those thoughts! How he would want to run away and hide, if all the world were to see the basket opened and see his thoughts![1]

Compared to the thoughts of God, we humans seem so frail. I can't imagine being exposed for the lowliness of my thoughts. I'm sometimes amazed that I could even think of such things. At times I think, "God, why did You permit that plane to crash, or why was it necessary for that murder to take place?" At times I want to crawl inside God's mind and see how it functions and how He thinks. Then I realize that He is the potter and I am the clay. His thoughts are so much higher than mine.

It must really be frustrating for a genius with a 200-plus IQ not to be able to outthink God. (I don't have that problem, since I'm nowhere near that level of thought!) But still I wonder about God's thought power.

In Philippians 4:8 Paul gives us some idea of God's level of thought process. He tells us to think on these things:

- Whatever is true
- Whatever is honorable
- Whatever is right
- Whatever is pure
- Whatever is lovely
- Whatever is of good report

If there is any excellence and if anything worthy of praise, let your mind dwell on these things. Then in verse 9 he gives us some action. What you have learned, received, heard, and seen in me—Practice these things. Then the God of peace will be with you.

As Christians we are all models that people watch to

see what God is like. They are watching and hearing what we have to say about life. Either they accept our level of thought or they reject it by what they have learned, received, heard, and seen in us.

We want to be a reflection of God: As people see us in action, do they see what this Christian walk is all about? Do our children and those around us ask, "Have I ever seen a Christian?" Or do they know absolutely that they have seen a Christian when they look at us?

If people were to find our "thought basket" on the wayside, what kind of flowers would they pull out?

*Father God, thank You for challenging me in this area of thoughts. Let me focus on pure thoughts that will stimulate me to be more Christlike. When I have a choice between two levels of thought, give me the strength and courage to take the higher road. Help women who read today's thoughts to be challenged to think upon the good things of life. May we all raise our level of thought. Amen.*

# Stop and Come

**Scripture Reading:** Genesis 22:1-18
**Key Verse:** Genesis 22:8

*Abraham answered, "God himself will provide*
*the lamb for the burnt offering, my son."*
*And the two of them went on together.*

There were two words we were firm about teaching our children when they were growing up: "Stop" and "Come." If you think about it, you probably use these words often with your own children. Children who learn them will be obedient people. I can honestly say the one thing our children learned was obedience. It has and is paying off, even in their adult lives.

Abraham is a beautiful example of obedience to his Father God. God tested Abraham to the limit of obedience. God called his name, "Abraham." Abraham *stopped* and replied, "Here I am, Lord." Then God instructed Abraham to take his only son to Moriah. There Abraham was to sacrifice Isaac as a burnt offering on one of the mountains. I wonder what Abraham thought. He loved Isaac so much. Isaac was the son of Sarah, who had prayed for many years for a child. Sarah had been in her nineties when she gave birth. Isaac was a miracle child, so wanted and so loved. Abraham knew God intimately. He had experienced the mighty power of God when He gave them Isaac in their later years. Now God was telling Abraham to sacrifice Isaac.

Early in the morning after God spoke to Abraham, Abraham took Isaac, saddled up his donkey, and along with two servants headed up to the mountain in Moriah. After cutting enough wood for the burnt offering, they set out as God had told him. "On the third day Abraham looked up and saw the place in the distance. He said to his servants, 'Stay here with the donkey while I and the boy go over there. *We* will worship and then *we* will come back to you'" (Genesis 22:5, emphasis added).

"*We* will worship. *We* will come back." Abraham believed God. He trusted God, and he kept moving ahead in obedience to God. I'm sure the servants and Isaac were puzzled. Where was the sacrifice? The servants didn't ask. Isaac didn't ask.

"Abraham took the wood for the burnt offering and placed it on his son Isaac, and he himself carried the fire and the knife" (verse 6). Isaac obviously wasn't a small child—he was big enough to carry heavy wood up a mountain. So I would guess he was probably pre- or early teens.

As father and son walked up the mountain, they probably talked together. "Isaac spoke up and said to his father Abraham, 'Father?' 'Yes my son,' Abraham replied. 'The fire and the wood are here,' Isaac said, 'but where is the lamb for the burnt offering?'" (verse 7). I'm sure Isaac was a bit puzzled. *We have everything but the lamb,* he may have thought. *Where will we ever find a lamb up here in the wilderness?*

I love Abraham's reply: "God himself will provide the lamb for the burnt offering, my son" (verse 8). And the two of them went on together. When they reached the place God had told Abraham about, he went to work, removing the wood from Isaac's back. He built an altar for worship and then arranged the wood on top. This was the ultimate of worshiping God—an altar built by hand and an offering of obedience.

Then Abraham said, "Come," to Isaac, and he placed him on top of the wood and bound him on the altar. Isaac was also obedient. He must have learned this from Abraham. Isaac came to his own father whom he loved and trusted—his father who loved and trusted Father God. While the Bible doesn't say anything about Isaac's words or thoughts, I'm sure he was very frightened. But perhaps he knew, too, that God would provide. Maybe Isaac was willing to die for God. I don't know, but there was Isaac—bound on top of the wood he had carried himself.

Abraham had the knife. Everything was prepared and ready. "Then [Abraham] reached out his hand and took the knife to slay his son" (verse 10). When an animal is sacrificed as an offering to God, it is bound on the altar of wood and the knife is plunged into the throat and sliced down the middle through the stomach. Abraham's arm was lifted up, ready to plunge the knife into his only son's throat when "the angel of the LORD called out to him from heaven 'Abraham! Abraham!'" (verse 11). Abraham *stopped.* "'Do not lay a hand on the boy,' he said. 'Do not do anything to him. Now I know that you fear God, because you have not withheld from me your son, your only son.' Abraham looked up and there in a thicket he saw a ram caught by its horns. He went and took the ram and sacrificed it as a burnt offering instead of his son" (verses 12-13). I'm sure Isaac must have thought, *That was a close call, Dad.*

Abraham named that place on top of the mountain "The Lord Will Provide." There was no doubt in Abraham's heart that God would provide. Can you imagine what the two servants must have thought when they saw Abraham and Isaac come back with no wood and a bloodstained knife? But then Abraham did say, "*We* will return." They did worship, and they did return. I know my worship today is stronger because of this passage. I'm sure Abraham and Isaac's was as well.

Isaac showed obedience when his father said, "*Come* with me to worship," and "*Come* get on the pile of wood." Abraham showed obedience, and he experienced in a truly deep and unique way that the Lord will provide. When the angel called his name, Abraham stopped to listen.

Perhaps our cup needs to be filled with an obedience like Abraham's. We say we trust God, but then we take matters into our own hands and try to move ahead in our own power, not allowing the Lord to provide. We miss seeing and experiencing the miracle hand of God.

What are you asking God to provide for you today? Job, children, husband, finances? Are you willing to trust Him and know He will provide? How obedient are we to God's call? Come! Come to His altar and lay the pain of your heart there. Stop and worship. And as you walk away from your worship with God, you will know with hope and trust that God says, "I will provide."

*Father God, You always surprise me with your*
*actions. It's hard to understand the mysterious*
*ways in which You work. All You ever ask is that*
*we trust and obey! May I "come" when You say*
*come and "stop" when You say stop. Amen.*

# Blessed Assurance

**Scripture Reading:** Psalm 37:1-40
**Key Verse:** Psalm 37:1-40 (NASB)

*Read and meditate on each verse today.*

*I* don't know if you're anything like me, but when I look at the local news events on television and in the newspaper, I see very little hope for the future. I get concerned for my children and grandchildren, and even for my great-grandchildren. I see a moral decay from what I cherished by being raised in the fifties. When I go by a high school, visit a mall, listen to the music of the youth, see the art of the masses, or witness the violence of the movies, I scream in my soul, STOP!

Then the Lord brings before me Psalm 37. In this passage David exhorts the righteous to trust in the Lord. Even when it looks like evil will overpower righteousness, God never abandons His children (verse 25). Though they may experience the heartaches of a sinful, fallen world, God's children are never forsaken. In fact, His blessings will extend to the next generation (verse 26).

41

During my quiet time with the Lord in this particular psalm, certain key phrases comfort my soul:

- *Do not fret,* be not envious (verse 1).
- *Trust* in the Lord, cultivate faithfulness (verse 3).
- *Delight* yourself in the Lord, He will give you abundantly (verse 4).
- *Commit* your way to Him, trust also in Him (verse 5).
- *Rest* in the Lord, wait patiently (verse 7).
- *Cease* from anger, do not fret (verse 8).
- The *humble* will inherit the land (verse 11).
- *Depart* from evil (verse 27).
- *Wait* for the Lord (verse 34).

Then in verses 39 and 40 we read of the great blessings we receive as children of God: "The salvation of the righteous is from the LORD; He is our strength in time of trouble. And the LORD helps them and delivers them; He delivers them from the wicked and saves them, because they take refuge in Him."

### I'm Drinking from the Saucer

...If God gives me strength and courage, when the way grows steep and rough, I'll not ask for other blessings—I'm already blessed enough. And may I never be too busy, to help another bear his load. Then I'll keep drinking from my saucer, 'Cause my cup has overflowed!

—JOHN PAUL MOORE

As I leave my prayer closet I am again able to face the negative issues of the day because David took time centuries ago to write this poetic psalm of comfort.

*Father God, again You come to comfort me in today's psalm. You give me assurance that righteousness does deflect evil, and that Your promises are as true today as they were centuries ago. Let me dwell on these significant words from this passage: trust, delight, commit, rest, be humble, wait. I ask that You give comfort to the ladies today as they bring their cares to You. Amen.*

# The Work of
# Our Hands

**Scripture Reading:** Psalm 90:12-17

**Key Verse:** Psalm 90:17b

*Confirm for us the work of our hands; yes,*
*confirm the work of our hands.*

For many years I struggled with the idea of worth in my work. I didn't have an advanced college degree and I was a homemaker with five children. I was always tired, with little energy for anything else—including romancing my husband. I didn't have a good handle on who I was as a person. I found myself saying to myself:

- You aren't worth much.
- You didn't have a career.
- Your job is so mundane.
- Anyone can do what you do.
- I don't have enough energy to do anything else.
- I'm stuck in a rat race with no place to go.

Over and over these thoughts went through my head. As you can suspect, I wasn't too exciting to be around!

I'm sure many readers of today's passage feel they have little worth in their hands. They have been browbeaten into thinking that life is fleeting by and they are being left behind. During this period in my life I was involved in a small Bible study with a few godly women who shared with us young ladies two passages of Scripture that changed my life.

One was Proverbs 31, which talked about the virtuous woman, and the other was Titus 2:4-5, which describes a wife's core role as "husband lover" and "child lover." These two sections of Scripture gave me the tools I needed to establish priorities and roles in making lifestyle decisions. I soon realized that this whole concept of work and worth was very complex and that there was no right answer to fit all situations. I realized that each woman and each family has to determine what is best for them, using biblical guidelines.

As I looked at Titus 2:4-5, I realized that God wanted me to be a lover of my husband and children. This was refreshing to me because I had looked at all these drudgeries as an end unto themselves, not as a means to fulfilling one of my primary roles as a woman. But now I found my attitude toward this work changing. I was beginning to do it out of love rather than obligation.

Once you see, you appreciate and then you become inspired.

—Alexandria Stoddard

I also realized that I did more than fulfill this role, but the role gave me some structure and direction. Up to this point in our marriage I had been experiencing frustration and disappointment because I had no direction in marriage.

The Proverbs 31 passage also made me realize that the ideal Hebrew woman handled many activities outside the home. But even while these extra activities were going on she remained focused on her husband, children, and home. Her husband can trust her, the passage says, because "she does him good and not evil all the days of her life" (verse 12).

With this new information I began to shift my focus from simply doing tasks to becoming a lover of my husband and children. To this day my core focus remains in this area of my life. Even though I have gone way beyond those early beginnings, I come across countless women who don't know about or aren't willing to perform the basic focus for a married woman: being a lover of their husband and children.

When I began to change my focus, I began to realize what today's key verse, Psalm 90:17b, was addressing: "Confirm for us the work of our hands; yes, confirm the work of our hands."

What's in it for me as a woman? Proverbs 31:28-29 gives me my blessing: "Her children rise up and bless her; her husband also, and he praises her, saying, 'Many daughters have done nobly, but you excel them all.'"

When my children and husband rise up and call me blessed, then I truly know that many years ago I made the right choice when I decided to be a lover of my husband and children. Without a doubt I know that God has confirmed the work of my hands.

*Father God, thank You again for sending me
Titus women at a young age to help me focus
my role as a wife and mother. As I stand before
You today I'm assured that I made the right
decision. I know that many women are confused
about their role as a woman. May they somehow
grasp this lifesaving concept of being a lover of
their husband and children first, and then other
opportunities will be opened to them. Amen.*

# Your Family in Christ

**Scripture Reading:** Ephesians 3:14-21
**Key Verse:** Ephesians 3:17-19

*And I pray that you, being rooted and established in love,
may have power, together with all the saints, to grasp how
wide and long and high and deep is the love of Christ,
and to know this love that surpasses knowledge—that you
may be filled to the measure of all the fullness of God.*

An old European story tells of a traveler in Germany who saw a peculiar sight in a tavern where he had stopped for dinner. After the meal, the tavern owner put a great bowl of soup on the floor and gave a loud whistle. A big dog, a large cat, an old raven, and a very large rat came into the room. They all four went to the dish and, without disturbing each other, ate together. After they had dined, the dog, cat, and rat lay before the fire, while Mr. Raven, in his black coat, hopped around the room. The tavern owner had trained these animals so that not one of them bothered to hurt any of the others.

He thought that if a dog, a rat, a cat, and a bird can live happily together, little children, especially brothers and sisters, ought to be able to do the same.

Yes, you would think that harmony could be established in our families, but somehow it escapes us.

In today's passage we find that through Paul's prayer we can learn some basic principles for praying for our own family.

1. *Pray that your family may be rooted and established in love.* Oh, how we need families that really love each other. We see so much evil that originates from the family. Ask God to protect your family from evil and put a big hedge of protection around each member. Continually be on guard for the wolf that tries to enter in and devour members of your family.

2. *Pray that you may have power to grasp how wide and long and high and deep is the love of Christ.* Today there is a lack of commitment, a lack of trust, a lack of love in relationships. Pray that your family may begin to grasp the vastness in Christ's love for them individually and collectively.

3. *Pray that your family may know this love that surpasses knowledge.* We cannot comprehend this love that gives beyond our knowledge. But with a great leap of faith, we believe and live the gospel message first within our own life and then share with our family members this love. There are two things to do with the gospel: one, we believe it; two, we live it.

4. *Pray that you will be filled in measure of all the fullness of God.* Each day that I'm in God's Word, I better understand what the fullness of God is all about. After many years of life, I better understand being filled in measure of God's fullness. And being in His family is so much a part of that fullness. Proverbs 24:3-4 states, "By wisdom a house is built, and through understanding it is established; through knowledge its rooms are filled with rare and beautiful treasures."

I will pray for you and your family, that you may grasp these principles and that your rooms will be filled with rare and beautiful treasures.

*Father God, You know that sometimes we have tensions in our family and we're not as united as we should be. I earnestly pray that we are rooted and established in love, and that we might realize how wide, how long, how high, and how deep Your love is for us. Grant me this supplication for my family. Amen.*

# Where Can Wisdom Be Found?

**Scripture Reading:** Job 28:12-22

**Key Verse:** Job 28:12 (NASB)

*Where can wisdom be found?*

*N*ot long ago my friend Florence Littauer wrote a book titled *Looking for Love in All the Wrong Places.* We are a culture which has a difficult time in reading the instruction manual. For some reason we want to invent the wheel by ourselves; we have trouble seeking the truth from the wise. We look for love in the wrong places, and we also seek wisdom in places where there is no wisdom. We talk to friends, read magazines, listen to talk shows, and attend seminars—all the wrong places.

The writer of the book of Job struggled with this same question of life. In Job 28:12 he asked, "Where can wisdom be found?" He too was perplexed with this question. All through chapter 28 he searched for the answer.

- Man doesn't know its value (verse 13a).
- It is not found in the land of the living (verse 13b).

- The inner earth says, "It's not in me" (verse 14a).

- The sea says, "It's not in me" (verse 14b).

- You can't buy it with gold or silver (verse 15).

- Precious stones don't have it (verse 16).

- It can't be equated with gold (verse 17).

- Pearls don't have it (verse 18).

- It is hidden from the eyes of all living creatures (verse 21a).

- Birds of the sky don't have it (verse 21b).

- Destruction and death say, "We have heard about it with our ears" (verse 22).

- God understands its way and He knows its place (verse 23).

- God looks to the ends of the earth and sees everything under heaven (verse 24).

- God saw wisdom and declared it (verse 27a).

- God established it and searched it out (verse 27b).

- In verse 28 God told man, "Behold, the fear of the Lord, that is wisdom" (showing holy respect and reverence for God and shunning evil).

Job and his friends claimed wisdom of themselves, but wisdom is clearly an outgrowth of God and not merely something to be obtained. Although we can know and understand many things, we cannot attain to the level of Creator-wisdom. There will always be unanswered questions, for which only God the Creator will know the answer. Solomon knew that true wisdom is not found in human understanding but is from God alone (Proverbs 1:7; 9:10).

I challenge you to learn this basic truth of Scripture. If you want to know God's perspective, read your Bible daily; don't look in all the wrong places for your answers in life. Start with the manual that tells you step-by-step how to live life.

In John 10:10 we are told that Jesus came so we could have abundant lives. May our lives be richly blessed because of our faithfulness to the Scriptures. We don't have to wonder if God will trust us with His wisdom; the good news throughout Scripture is that the Lord gives wisdom liberally and without reproach to all of us who ask Him (James 1:5-6). If we approach the Lord in faith to show us what to do, what to say, and how to live, we can count on Him to give us His wisdom.

*Father God, thank You for revealing to me
where the true source of wisdom comes from. I
truly want to show holy respect and reverence
for You. As I read Your Word daily, I pray
that Your truths will pop out to me and that
I will continue to seek Your wisdom. May I*

never get to the point where I think I know
everything about You. Thank You, Lord,
for continuing to work in my life. Amen.

# Three Loves

**Scripture Reading:** Deuteronomy 6:4-9

**Key Verse:** Deuteronomy 6:5

*Love the LORD your God with all your heart and with all your soul and with all your strength.*

Today's Scripture talks about three basic loves:

- Love for God
- Love for your neighbor
- Love for yourself

Our circle of love is full when we are able to love in this way. The whole world would know of Jesus if the Christians in the church would manifest these three basic love relationships. Our passage challenges us by giving a directive to:

- Put these commandments in our hearts.
- Impress them on our children.
- Talk about them continually.
- Tie them as symbols on our bodies.
- Write them on our door frames and gates.

God must be serious about this because He engulfs our lives with continuous reminders of His commandments to love.

How do we manifest these three loves? Paul, in writing to the church at Ephesus, includes a section on a believer's relationship with the Holy Spirit, beginning in Ephesians 5:18: "Instead, be filled with the Spirit." In the verses that follow we learn that we are to be satisfied with self, God, and others.

If we are satisfied with ourselves, Paul teaches us to manifest it in speaking and singing words of joy: "Speak to one another with psalms, hymns, and spiritual songs. Sing and make music in your heart to the Lord" (verse 19). Satisfied lives will be ones of joy, praise, and excitement. They will reflect positive thoughts, ideas, and praises to God. What a great test to see where our personal satisfaction is! Are we known as a person who is fun to be around or as someone who people avoid? God wants us to be satisfied with ourselves and reflect the joy of the Lord in our soul, mind, and spirit.

Paul continues in verse 20, "Always giving thanks for all things in the name of our Lord Jesus Christ to God, even the Father" (NASB). This verse shows *our* satisfaction with *God*. If we are satisfied, we find ourselves giving thanks for all things. We have an appreciative heart for all that goes on around us. The positive words flow from our lips unto God.

Our third satisfaction is with other people. In verse

21 Paul teaches, "And be subject to one another in the fear of Christ." As women, we find that when we love God and ourselves, we become equipped to be submissive to others. These words, "subject" or "submissive," unfortunately, have taken a beating in today's culture. In essence, these words are telling us to be satisfied with other people to the point that we are willing to step aside in our personal relationships. We are willing to allow another's needs to take precedence over our own. The submission is to be mutual among Christians, among husband and wife, and based on reverence for God. It is impossible to be subject to one another by human desire. It is possible only when we mutually submit to one another out of respect for God.

Ephesians 5:18-21 truly gives us guidelines for being satisfied with God, with ourselves, and with others.

As I have taught this concept over the years, I have used a diagram to illustrate my point:

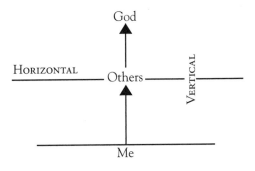

As you can see, we have vertical and horizontal relationships. The vertical relationship is between God and me, and the horizontal relationship is between other people and me. I find that when God and I have the proper relationship, my relationship with others falls into proper alignment. If I have dissatisfaction with myself and others, I realize that I am not responding to God properly. Over the years, God has taught me to put first things first: to love God, to love self, and to love others.

*Father God, life is so difficult at times. There seems to be so many things pulling at me that I get exhausted trying to be all things to all people. Let me start each day concentrating on the three loves. It seems so basic, but I know it takes a lifetime to accomplish. Amen.*

# Look to the Left,
# Look to the Right

**Scripture Reading:** Matthew 9:35-38
**Key Verse:** Matthew 9:36 (NASB)

*He felt compassion for them, because they were distressed
and downcast like sheep without a shepherd.*

ach new day as I exit my front door and look to the left and to the right I find the world full of people who are distressed and downcast.

As I watch the morning news on my favorite TV channel I hear nothing but stories of people who are in distress and are downcast. As my Bob and I eat breakfast and go over the morning newspaper we are stunned by the articles in the paper:

- Pakistan blast kills 40
- Tens of thousands of Brazilians are reported toiling in bondage
- Boy six years old arrested for assaulting a month-old baby to near-death

- Gunman caught after killing 33 in Australia
- Apartment fire leaves 12 dead in Tijuana
- Bus bombed in protest of election; 15 dead
- Bus crash kills 31
- Trials set in killings of Brazilian street children
- $20 million frees abducted millionaire
- Zulu princess' body found at soccer field

After reading all of these depressing headlines, it's hard for us to finish eating breakfast. Yes, the world is full of people who are distressed and downcast.

In our passage for today we find Jesus teaching in all the cities and villages and proclaiming the good news of the gospel. As He looked at the multitudes He felt compassion for them. Yet in today's culture of violence we become desensitized to all the bad news we see, read, and hear. If it doesn't affect us and our friends we have a tendency to turn our heads and look the other way.

Maybe instead of looking to the left and to the right we should look *up toward God* and utter a prayer for all of those caught up in distress. We can't always do anything about people in foreign countries who face terrible problems, but we can look around and find people close to us in similar situations. Ask God to show you people you can help who face such dilemmas.

As Jesus showed compassion to those around Him, we too should show compassion. John Andrew Holmes is credited with saying, "There is no exercise better for the heart than reaching down and lifting people up."

This could mean a love basket of food, payment of a utility bill, a phone call of encouragement, babysitting while the person looks for a job, or a note saying you are praying for their situation.

Let's go beyond our comfort zone today and lift someone up who is down!

*Father God, let me become aware of people in my immediate surroundings who are distressed and downcast. I'm not by nature a compassionate person, but let me today take on one of Jesus' character traits: compassion. I thank You for what You are doing in my life regarding concern for others. Amen.*

# Your Most Important Decision

**Scripture Reading:** Joshua 24:14-15
**Key Verse:** Joshua 24:15

*But as for me and my household,
we will serve the LORD.*

Some decisions we make in life are everlasting. We see throughout history how proper and improper decisions have changed the history of mankind.

Joshua faced the same dilemma for his family as we do for our family. Which God to worship? The gods of the world or *the* God—Jehovah?

Choosing whom to worship is the most basic question of our life. Joshua was a man of courage, strength, determination, and faith. He was a leader to his family and nation. As recorded in today's Scripture reading, Joshua states that we worship the gods we want to. For Joshua and his family, they will serve the Lord.

Which of the gods will you serve? Your life today is a consequence of the decisions you made yesterday.

Are you tired of being a slave to poor decisions of the past? If so, you can have the freedom and joy of being in Christ. You do not have to continue to suffer the pain of yesterday; today you can commit to turning your life around.

Paul writes in Romans 10:9-10, "That if you confess with your mouth, 'Jesus is Lord,' and believe in your heart that God raised him from the dead, you will be saved. For it is with your heart that you believe and are justified, and it is with your mouth that you confess and are saved."

Can you make a decision today about this promise? It will be the best decision of your life. Don't delay. Don't wait until it's too late. The writer of Ecclesiastes 3:1 states, "There is a time for everything, and a season for every activity under heaven."

Three times a soldier in a hospital picked up the hymn "Will You Go?" which was scattered as a tract. Twice he threw it down. The last time, he read it, thought about it, and, taking his pencil, wrote deliberately in the margin these words: "By the grace of God, I will try to go, John Waugh, Company G, Tenth Regiment, P.R.V.C." That night, he went to a prayer meeting, read his resolution, requested prayers for his salvation, and said, "I am not ashamed of Christ now; but I am ashamed of myself for having been so long ashamed of Him." He was killed a few months later. How timely was his resolution!

Today is the appointed time. Make that decision for the first time, or reconfirm a previous decision that you and your family will serve the Lord.

*Father God, each day I must choose what god I will worship. May I, as Joshua did, choose Jehovah God. I want to serve You with all my heart and soul. Please renew that desire in me on a daily basis. I love You. Amen.*

# Use Wisely What He Has Given You

**Scripture Reading:** Matthew 25:14-30
**Key Verse:** Matthew 25:29 (NASB)

*To everyone who has shall more be given, and he shall
have an abundance; but from the one who does not
have, even what he does have shall be taken away.*

God has given each of us specific talents—to some
more than others, but to each of us *something*. What
kind of stewards are we to become in using these talents?
Some of us know from personal experience how a stut-
tering child can become an eloquent speaker and how a
brilliant debater can become homeless when he uses his
talent slothfully.

In today's passage we find Jesus telling His disciples
that the kingdom of heaven is like a man who called his
servants to delegate to them a portion of his property.
To one servant he gave five gold coins, to another two

coins, and to the third one coin. Each servant was given according to his ability.

The first man traded with his five coins and made five more. The man with two coins did likewise and made two more. But the one-coin man dug a hole in the ground and buried it.

After awhile the owner of the land came to settle the accounts with his three servants. The first servant brought with him the original five coins plus five additional ones. The master said, "Well done, good and faithful slave; you were faithful with a few things, I will put you in charge of many things" (verse 21).

The second man, who had been given just two coins, brought forth the original two plus the two he had made. The master likewise said, "Well done, good and faithful slave; you were faithful with a few things, I will put you in charge of many things; enter into the joy of your master" (verse 23).

The third servant came forward with the one gold coin and said, "Master, I knew you to be a hard man, reaping where you did not sow and gathering where you scattered no seed. And I was afraid and went away and hid your talent in the ground; see, you have what is yours" (verses 24-25).

But the master replied, "You wicked, lazy slave, you knew that I reap where I did not sow and gather where I scattered no seed. Then you ought to have put my money in the bank, and on my arrival I would have received my money back with interest. Therefore take away the talent from him and give it to the one who has the ten talents" (verses 26-28).

Then Jesus stated, "For to everyone who has shall more be given, and he shall have an abundance; but from the one who does not have, even what he does have shall be taken away" (verse 29).

This third man didn't mean any harm to the master, but he didn't understand the principles of stewardship and faithfulness. When we are faithful we are reliable: appearing on time, doing what we say we are going to do, finishing the job we started, and being there when we need to be there.

Everyday life operates on the laws of faith and trust. We assume that people are going to honor their word, stop at red lights, pay monthly mortgage payments, pay the utility bills, show up for an appointment, be faithful in marriage. Throughout Scripture God shows His attribute of being faithful.

We need women who will reach out with one or two or five talents and invest them wisely in their home, marriage, church, family, and community. We need women who will take the little they have and double it so that when we stand before Jesus He will say, "Well done, good and faithful servant; enter into the joy of my father's mansions." What a glorious day that will be!

*Father God, I live in a world of comparisons, and I only see people who have five talents, while You seem to have neglected me by giving me only one. I feel, "how can I be as good as that person, since she has so much more than I do?" I pray that You would clearly show me how I can be faithful to the one talent that I have. Thank You, Lord, for all You have given to me. Amen.*

# Not Ashamed
## of the Gospel

**Scripture Reading:** Romans 1:1-17
**Key Verse:** Romans 1:16

*I am not ashamed of the gospel, because it is the power of God for the salvation of everyone who believes; first for the Jew, then for the Gentile.*

*A*shamed of the gospel of Christ! Let the skeptic, let the wicked profligate, blush at his deeds of darkness, which will not bear the light, lest they should be made manifest; but never let the Christian blush to own the holy gospel. Where is the philosopher who is ashamed to own the God of Nature? Where is the Jew that is ashamed of Moses? or the Moslem that is ashamed of Mahomet? and shall the Christian, and the Christian minister, be ashamed of Christ? God forbid! No! Let me be ashamed of myself, let me be ashamed of the world, and let me blush at sin; but never, never, let me be ashamed of the gospel of Christ!"[2]

Dr. R. Newton was passionate in his plea of not

being ashamed of the gospel. As I reflect upon my life, I have to confess that I have had an easy time of sharing the gospel due to the religious climate in America over the years. Lately, however, I have begun to realize that the religious freedom of the past may not be the same freedom of the future.

In our passage today, we see seven principles about the gospel that Paul is trying to teach the believers in Rome—and to us.

*Point 1: We are all set apart for the gospel* (verse 1). What an awesome thought that we are set apart! That makes us something special in the sight of God. With this thought, it helps me establish my daily priorities. It's not sports, politics, knowledge, business, or finances, but the gospel that goes to the top of the list.

*Point 2: This gospel was promised beforehand through His prophets in the Holy Scripture* (verse 2). I must realize that this precious gospel has a historical background that has been documented in the Bible. It's not something that was just recently thought up by a group of men in a dark back room.

*Point 3: We are to share the gospel with our whole heart* (verse 9). With a passion and a zeal we are to share this good news with our friends and acquaintances.

*Point 4: We are to share this good news with everyone* (verses 14-15). Paul says he was obligated and eager to preach the gospel to both the Greeks and non-Greeks, to the wise and to the foolish—to the whole spectrum of life. The message of Jesus can make a difference in anyone's life.

*Point 5: We are to take a stand for the gospel* (verse 16). Paul very powerfully states, "I am not ashamed of the gospel." Oh, do we ever need individuals and families who can stand together and exhibit a lifestyle that reflects the love of Christ. We need to show the world that we aren't ashamed of this gospel.

*Point 6: We need to see the power of the gospel for salvation* (verse 16). This gospel is a change agent, giving people real purpose and meaning to life, helping us struggle against the power of sin. Each of us not only knows of this miracle in our own lives, but also in the testimonies of those around us.

*Point 7: We are to live a life of righteousness by faith* (verse 17). In studying the gospel, the righteousness of God is revealed to us, so we can go out and live a righteous life by the power of the Holy Spirit.

May today's study help us focus on the eternal values of life and not only the temporal. There are a lot of good things to use up our energies and passions, but are they the best priorities for our time and energy? One of our Barnes mottos is: "Say 'No' to good things and save our 'Yeses' for the best." Know what's important and act on it.

*Father God, help me be obedient and give witness
to Your Son when the opportunity arises. Amen.*

# Christians Are to Persevere

**Scripture Reading:** James 1:2-8
**Key Verse:** James 1:4 (NASB)

*Let endurance have its perfect result, that you may
be perfect and complete, lacking in nothing.*

*A* hare was one day making fun of a tortoise for
being so slow on his feet. "Wait a bit," said the tortoise; "I'll run a race with you, and I'll wager that I win."
"Oh, well," replied the hare, who was much amused at
the idea, "let's try it and see." They agreed that the fox
should set a course for them and be the judge. When the
time for the race came, both started off together, but the
hare was soon so far ahead that he thought he might as
well have a rest; so he lay down and fell fast asleep. The
tortoise, meanwhile, kept plodding on, and in time he
reached the goal. At last the hare woke up with a start
and dashed on at his fastest, only to find that the tortoise
had already won the race. —Adapted from Aesop

Too many of us only see the start of the race and aren't

around to see the end and find out who the real winners are. So much of life is painted with speed, flash, and sizzle that we get intimidated by everyone else's flash.

A few years ago our family went to Lake Tahoe to snow ski during the Christmas break. As I walked on the icy slopes of this beautiful resort my eyes were full of the best: the best of cars, of ski racks, of clothing, of beauty, of laughter. I couldn't believe my eyes—I had never seen so much sizzle in one place. Everyone was perfect!

So I said to myself, "No way am I going to compete with them." But after being coaxed into my group ski lesson I found that many of the "sizzle group" were also in my class and that they couldn't ski any better than I could!

The Scripture for today teaches that perseverance is *enduring with patience*. We will experience many trials in life that can discourage and defeat us. In the Bible, "perseverance" is a term used to describe Christians who faithfully endure and remain steadfast in the face of opposition, attack, and discouragement. When we persevere with patience, we exhibit our ability to endure without complaint and with calmness.

As believers we need to daily commit ourselves to godly living. Our daily commitments lead us to lasting discipline. I tell my ladies at our seminars, "It takes only 21 consecutive days to create a new habit."

*Commitment* and *discipline* are not words that the world is comfortable with. We want everything to feel good, and these words don't always feel good. They are words that demand denial of self and pain. "Feeling good" people don't like pain or testing; it makes them very uncomfortable, particularly when they don't trust the Tester.

Scripture is very clear when it teaches that we are to persevere—

- in prayer (Ephesians 6:18);
- in obedience (Revelation 14:12);
- in faith (Hebrews 12:1-2);
- in service (1 Corinthians 15:58);
- in self-control (2 Peter 1:5-7).

Scripture promises us certain blessings if we endure till the end—final deliverance (Matthew 24:13), rewarded faith (Hebrews 11:6), and eternal inheritance (Revelation 21:7). As we live out this life daily and are able to persevere in all its trials and temptations, we will be rewarded by the Lord with the fruit of His Spirit now and for all eternity (Galatians 5:22-23): love, goodness, joy, faithfulness, peace, gentleness, patience, self-control, and kindness.

*Father God, please open my eyes to see that life is a laboratory that is developing Christian character in my life. Let me not get sidetracked*

*by all the hares of life. I want to stay true to You during all the ups and downs of daily living. In life's difficulties I want to look heavenward to see what You are trying to teach me in these particular situations. May I always be faithful to Your Word. Amen.*

# Declare God's Power and Might

**Scripture Reading:** Psalm 71:14-18
**Key Verse:** Psalm 71:18

*Even when I am old and gray, do not forsake
me, O God, till I declare your power to the next
generation, your might to all who are to come.*

As I get older, I think more and more about what
comes next. I know there's got to be something else
after this life is over, because I can't grasp the alternative. I can't imagine that through all eternity I'll never
see anyone I love again, that my whole awareness will
just be obliterated. I can't believe that we're only bodies
passing through.

I've always marveled at how belief in the hereafter
gets accentuated as people grow older. Until their deathbeds, many of the great minds in science thought that
because their soul and being were wrapped up in their
body—the old ninety-eight cents' worth of chemicals—
and that because after death these would no longer

be a body, that was it. But now when they have to go, suddenly they want to believe in somebody up there because they don't know where they're going and they are scared.[3]

There is a season of life which challenges our belief of the hereafter. What happens when we die? The psalmist pleads for God not to forsake him until he declares the power of God to the next generation. Wow! What a great prayer. I guess that's why I do what I do. I want to tell everyone, starting with my immediate family and branching out to others, about the power and the might of God.

Lord, I have so much to tell. Just continue to give me a message, give me a passion for the message, give me power to tell the message, and give me an audience who wants to hear the message.

One of my favorite passages that gives me a vision for that all-important message is found in Titus 2:3-6: "Likewise, teach the older women to be reverent in the way they live, not to be slanderers or addicted to much wine, but to teach what is good. Then they can train the younger women to love their husbands and children, to be self-controlled and pure, to be busy at home, to be kind, and to be subject to their husbands, so that no one will malign the word of God."

If only we could grasp the vastness of these words. And some say that being a wife and homemaker isn't exciting and challenging!

Don't wait until you are old and gray-haired. Begin today to share the message of Jesus Christ with the whole world.

Perhaps you're unsure of the message. Read this chain of Scripture to gain God's revelations for salvation.

- Romans 3:23
- Romans 6:23
- Acts 16:30-31
- Ephesians 2:8-9
- Romans 10:9-10
- Luke 18:13
- Luke 23:43
- John 10:28
- John 14:2-3

You can receive Christ right now by faith through prayer.

> *Lord Jesus, I need You. Thank You for dying on the cross for my sins. I open the door of my life and receive You as my Savior and Lord. Thank You for forgiving my sins and giving me eternal life. Take control of the throne of my life. Make me the kind of person You want me to be.*[4]

If you prayed this prayer, read the following Scriptures for your assurance.

- Revelation 3:20
- 1 John 5:11-13
- Hebrews 13:5
- John 14:21

# A Yielding of
# the Heart

**Scripture Reading:** Luke 1:46-56

**Key Verse:** Luke 1:52 (NASB)

*He has brought down rulers from their thrones,
and has exalted those who were humble.*

*I*n the New Testament we find the word "humility" to mean a personal quality of dependence on God and respect for other people. It is not a natural human instinct but is a God-given virtue acquired through holy living.

While the mind of the natural man is selfish and proud, the essence of Jesus' mind is unselfish and loving toward others. Christ was our great example of a proper walk: pleasing to God.

Our hearts must be transformed by the Holy Spirit so that we can reflect God's love to others through the humble example of Jesus.

Corrie ten Boom, an unbelievable Dutch woman who survived the horror of World War II while in the confines of the German death camps, received a lot of praise for what she did during her confinement, and yet she remained unfazed by all the tributes. When asked how she managed to stay so humble among all these honors she humbly replied, "I accept every compliment as a flower and say thank you, and each evening I put them in a bunch and lay them at Jesus' feet, where the praise belongs."

Our world is full of men and women who are eager to take God's honor and heap it on their own heads. But God has a way of humbling us. From my own experience in life I know that I need to come before His throne with open arms and humbly bow before Him, seeking whatever He has for my life. We all need to learn this lesson of humility in life, because God has promised that if we don't humble ourselves, He will do it for us.

To learn humility is to learn contentment in all circumstances. Humility is not in what we own or achieve, but in maintaining a teachable attitude, a willingness to bend to the will of the Father.

—JAN SILVIOUS

When Christ entered into the Greek world, they hated the quality of humility, but Jesus entered as a humble Savior. He became obedient to God's will, which led to His death on the cross. Throughout Jesus' walk on this earth He taught people to be humble before God and man.

In today's passage we see that God will exalt those who are humble. Humility comes from God and results in the praise of God.

*Father God, You know how I want to lay down my bouquet of flowers at Your feet and give You all the praise. I know I am nothing without You. You have taken an ordinary woman and exalted her to a point at which I don't feel adequate. Thank You for fulfilling Your promise in me. Through my life may You be richly praised and lifted up. I am humbled that You can use me in life. Let me touch people so they know they have seen and felt Jesus. Amen.*

# The Pain of Rejection

*For God so loved the world that he
gave his one and only Son.*

Oh, how often we have been rejected in our life! That first date, first marriage proposal, first college entrance application. That first promotion, that first home we didn't qualify for. We have all experienced the hurt and pain of rejection. Let your mind race quickly through that long list of rejections. We often cried. We sometimes called a close friend to let her know of our hurt. Our mom and dad heard our crying out to God, asking, "Why, why, why?"

Jesus faced the pain of rejection even unto death. The people He came to save were the very ones who nailed Him to the cross (John 1:10). Isaiah the prophet stated that the Messiah would be despised and rejected by men (Isaiah 53:3). Even knowing this outcome, Jesus bore the pain of rejection.

On the cross, Jesus shouted to God in heaven, "My

God, my God, why have you forsaken me?" (Matthew 27:46). Even His Father had rejected Him.

Jesus' life is a reflection of how He met this rejection:

- He never abandoned the mission that God had given to Him.

- He never fought against His tormentors.

- He responded in love.

Paul writes in Hebrews 4:15-16 that Jesus sympathizes with our weakness, that we may receive mercy and grace in our time of need. What a great Savior! He has experienced our pain and can help us.

Scripture has given us some tremendous promises to hang on to during times of rejection:

- "Never will I leave you, never will I forsake you" (Hebrews 13:5).

- "Praise be to God who comforts us in all our troubles, so that we can comfort those in any trouble with the comfort we ourselves have received from God" (2 Corinthians 1:3-4).

- "Having believed, you were marked in Him with a seal, the promised Holy Spirit" (Ephesians 1:13).

It's natural to dwell on the pain of rejection. You can choose bitterness, depression, anger, fear, doubt, or loneliness to dominate your life. But these negative emotions can destroy you. Don't let Satan get a foothold in your Christian growth. There is a better way—God's way. He asks you to forgive and to do good to those who hurt you. He knows these actions aren't just for the benefit of the one who hurt you, but for your benefit as well.

God set the model of forgiveness in Matthew 5:44-45 when He tells us to love our enemies and pray for those who persecute us.

It's only when we adopt His attitude that we can fully experience His healing of our hurts. If you've been hurt by the poison arrow of rejection, then for your own sake, forgive. This forgiveness prevents even greater pain.

When we respond to rejection with God's love, others will notice the difference. Some will be so moved that they will be drawn to Christ and be saved. God will be glorified, and you will experience the wonderful feeling of spiritual victory. It will not be easy, but it is always worth the effort.

Don't be dragged down to defeat. Let rejection be an opportunity to develop Christian character in your life.

*Father God, let my rejections be a step forward and not backward. You have something better for me. Amen.*

# There Was Only One

**Scripture Reading:** Luke 17:11-19

**Key Verse:** Luke 17:15 (NASB)

*One of them, when he saw that he had been healed,
turned back, glorifying God with a loud voice.*

*A*s a wife and mother who is dedicated to her family and really does things because of her love for them, there are times when I would like them to take a moment and loudly say, "Mmm, that was really a good dinner! Those peas are my favorite!" Or "Mom, thanks for washing my clothes so I always have something clean to wear to school." Have you ever longed for that token of thanks? All of us, regardless of what we do (bus driver, waitress, gardener, teacher), would like to hear "Thank you!"

I'm sure Jesus was no exception to our own human needs, since He became a man for us. He was hoping that of the ten men He had healed, more than one would come back and say, "Thank You, Jesus!" But only one came back, glorifying God with a loud voice. He was truly appreciative and knew that a miracle had been performed on him. This man also realized that an almighty God had performed this miracle, and He was going to be glorified.

I would love to have been a quiet mouse in the corner listening to the other nine men's excuses for not coming back to Jesus to say thanks. It might go like this:

- Leper number 1: Left to shop at Nordstrom's. He didn't have time.

- Leper number 2: Was late to play a round of golf. He didn't have time.

- Leper number 3: Had to rush home to mow the lawn. He didn't have time.

- Leper number 4: Had a sick grandmother and had to take her for a doctor's appointment. He didn't have time.

- Leper number 5: Had to get a haircut for church the next day. He didn't have time.

- Leper number 6: Had to take his son to a soccer game. He didn't have time.

- Leper number 7: Had to go back to the office to do some paperwork. He didn't have time.

- Leper number 8: Had to pick up a few groceries at the market. He didn't have time.

- Leper number 9: Was too embarrassed because

the majority of the men weren't going back. He didn't have time.

But thank God for leper number 10. He had time to go back and say, "Thank You, Jesus." Notice in verse 19 that Jesus said, "Rise and go your way; your faith has made you well." He was healed both physically and spiritually.

One of God's chief complaints against mankind is that they do not glorify Him as God, nor do they take the time to say "Thank You."

One of the ways we can give thanks to God for all His abundance is to have grace or a blessing at the dinner table. At an early age our children were aware that Mom and Dad took time to bless our food. As they got older they were given an opportunity to thank God in their own unique way. Our fourth grandchild, Bradley Joe, insists that we end our prayer with a catchy tune and words that say, "Amen, Amen, Amen, Amen, Amen."

A quiet time for individual or group devotions helps to instill in our family an awareness of God's blessings on our family. Somehow find your own unique way to show God that you and your family glorify Him and say thanks with a heartfelt enthusiasm.

*Father God, I want to respond as leper number*

*10 did and tell You how much I thank You for all You have done for me. I am so blessed to be one of Your children. May I never stop thanking You. You are my number one priority, and I want my life to reflect that in my daily living. Amen.*

# Humility —God's Characteristic

**Scripture Reading:** 1 Peter 5:5-11

**Key Verse:** 1 Peter 5:5b

*All of you, clothe yourselves with humility toward one another, because, "God opposes the proud but gives grace to the humble."*

$\mathcal{A}$s I walk past the Monday night football games on television, I see all kinds of strange dances. Most of them occur after a player has scored a touchdown. I can't help but think that a person doing such antics hasn't learned the first step in humility. I was always taught to let your skills do your talking and to act in a calm, reserved fashion. And it's not just football players on Monday night. The world has gone mad with pride.

I believe humility is a foundational character quality at the heart of every successful relationship. Those who exhibit great pride usually don't have strong interpersonal relationships.

Peter writes, "Clothe yourselves with humility

toward one another, because 'God opposes the proud, but gives grace to the humble.' Humble yourselves, therefore, under God's mighty hand, that he may lift you up in due time." In present-day management books we read about climbing the corporate ladder, upward mobility, self-assertion, moving on up. It's always *up*. However, God seems to have a different program. The way up with God is always *down*. Peter's exhortation to be "clothed with humility" is a command, not a mere suggestion. God opposes the proud. The moment we allow pride to raise its ugly head, the resistance of God begins.

In Psalm 16:5 we read, "The Lord detests all the proud of heart." God not only resists and opposes the proud, but He is clear in His teachings that the proud will be humbled. Proverbs 29:23 states, "A man's pride brings him low."

Peter teaches us this truth: When you are clothed with humility, God terminates His resistance against you. As God's children, we should be smart enough to stay on the good side of God by staying on the side of humility.

God always opposes the proud, yet if we are humble, He will exalt us at the proper time. "Humility comes before honor" (Proverbs 15:33). "Humble yourself before the Lord and He will lift you up" (James 4:10). "He has brought down rulers from their thrones, but has lifted up the humble" (Luke 1:52).

Then what is humility?

- It is moral realism, the result of a fresh revelation of God.

- It is esteeming others as better than ourselves.

- It is the fruit of repentance.

- It is the attitude that rejoices in the success of others.

- It is the freedom from having to be right.

- It is the foundation of unity.

- It is the mark of authenticity.

- It is the fruit of brokenness.

- It is the quality that catches the attention of God.

The end result is holiness. Our only response to God's holiness, and that of His Son Jesus, is humility. If you are interested in developing a long-term relationship with both God and others, make humility your goal. As we kneel at the foot of our Lord, He will lift us up.

*Father God, I want to be humble in all*
*that I say and do. Please make me aware*
*of any false pride in my life. Amen.*

# He Began a Good Work in You

**Scripture Reading:** Philippians 1:1-11
**Key Verse:** Philippians 1:6 (NASB)

*I am confident of this very thing, that He who began a good work in you will perfect it until the day of Christ Jesus.*

At one point in my young married career, I found my motivations to be all wrong. I really wanted to be a helpmate for Bob, but I was caught up in the pressure of trying to meet everyone's expectations, including my own. The house always had to be perfect and the children spotless. I was frustrated as a wife and mother because I was doing it all myself—100 percent from me and nothing from God. I was trying to be the perfect wife, perfect in every way. I was trying to be—loving, kind, a friend, patient, and well-organized.

In addition to all this

• I balanced discipline and flexibility

- my home was always neat and well-decorated
- my children were always well-behaved
- I was serious, but I could laugh
- I was submissive, but not passive
- I was full of energy and never tired
- my dress was proper and suitable for all occasions
- I could work in the garden without getting dirt under my fingernails
- I was always healthy
- and I had a close walk with God

Needless to say, I wasn't being very effective at anything I did. I had created a superwoman image that I couldn't pull off.

During this time in my life I came across Philippians 1:6: "I am confident of this very thing, that He who began a good work in you will perfect it until the day of Christ Jesus." I realized that I was the product of God working in me and that I had three alternatives for solving my dilemma: First, I could continue trying to be superwife and supermom by doing everything myself; second, I could follow the old adage "Let go and let God," and let God do everything; or third, I could enter a balanced partnership between myself and God.

I selected the last alternative because according to Philippians 2:12-13 God was at work inside me, helping me to obey Him and to do what He wanted. God had made me a wife and a mom on purpose, and He would help me perform my role. Once I accepted this truth, a burden lifted from my life. I experienced less stress and I had a better understanding of what God wanted from me and what resources He was able to provide me. The drudgeries of homemaking became a real joy when I saw myself as a partner with God in developing godly traits in my children and creating a warm, safe nest for our family.

As I searched the Scriptures to discover my role in this partnership, I came up with three areas.

1. *Faithfulness.* According to 1 Corinthians 4:2, if I am to be a good manager of my home, I must remain faithful. Specifically, God wants me to faithfully thank Him that His plans are being fulfilled in my family. I am often impatient and want things to change right now. But God wants me to stop being concerned about His timetable and to just give thanks that He is doing His job. Over the years I have learned that if I am faithful in giving thanks, God is faithful in His part.

2. *Obedience.* It is my responsibility to act upon God's promises for my life. I can't just sit back and do nothing. Nor can I wait until all situations are perfect and safe. I must do a good job of preparation and then move ahead obediently, even if it means risking failure. Some of my best steps of growth have come after failure.

3. *Growth.* When Bob and I attended Bill Gothard's seminar several years ago he was distributing a lapel

badge with the following initials: PBPGINFWMY. I was intrigued by the badge, and soon found out that the letters represented the simple message "Please be patient; God is not finished with me yet."

Yes, the Christian walk is a process of growth. I wanted to arrive instantly at the level of being a perfect wife and mother, but God showed me that my focus was to be on the lifelong process, not on arrival. If we focus on perfection we will always be disappointed because we will never achieve it. But if we focus on the process of growth we can always have hope for improvement tomorrow.

*Father God, thank You for revealing to me that life is a process. I don't have to be superwoman or some phantom wife that society has depicted for me. You know who I am, what strengths and weaknesses I possess, and that my goal is to serve You. Please reveal to me a balance in living out life. Help those women who are in a similar state of life today. Give them the power to overcome the forces of false expectations. Amen.*

# We Do What We Want to Do

**Scripture Reading:** Genesis 18:18-19
**Key Verse:** Genesis 18:19

*For I have chosen him, so that he will direct his children and his household after him to keep the way of the LORD by doing what is right and just, so that the LORD will bring about for Abraham what he has promised him.*

*M*y parents spent a lot of time with me, and I wanted my kids to be treated with as much love and care as I got. Well, that's a noble objective. Everyone feels that way. But to translate it into daily life, you really have to work at it.

Kathi was on the swim team for seven years, and I never missed a meet. Then there were tennis matches. I made all of them. And piano recitals. I made all of them too. I was always afraid that if I missed one, Kathi might finish first or finish last and I would hear about it secondhand and not be there to congratulate—or console—her.

People used to ask me: "How could somebody as busy as you go to all those swim meets and recitals?" I just put them down on my calendar as if I were seeing a supplier or a dealer that day. I'd write down: "Go to country club. Meet starts at three-thirty, ends four-thirty." And I'd zip out.[5]

We have to make so many choices in each of our twenty-four-hour days. How do we establish what's important? By reconfirming day by day what's of value to us. Our Scripture reading today makes us realize that as children of God we have been chosen and are directed by God to keep the way of the Lord by doing what is right and just. The Lord will bring about for you what He has promised you.

Do you really realize that you have been chosen by God? What a tremendous revelation! We are living in an age of irresponsibility, but as children of God we have responsibility. What are you doing to be directed by God? You can start by always having a teachable spirit. Since you are reading this book, I'm going to guess that you are a learner and want to grow. Each day choose to be a learner and to be directed by God to do what is right and just. We do what we want to do!

Notice that today's key verse points out that the reward for stewardship in the family is that the Lord will bring about what He has promised.

In Proverbs 24:3-4 we learn more about these promises: "By wisdom a house is built, and through understanding it is established; through knowledge its rooms are filled with rare and beautiful treasures." Is the writer of Proverbs talking about furniture, carpets, crystal, vases, paintings? I don't think so. These rare and beautiful treasures are God-fearing, God-respecting children, with good and moral values, children who honor their mother and father and respect others. God has promised these rewards and blessings if only we would abide by His directions. Begin today a new and renewed passion for God's direction in your life.

*Father God, let me build my house with
wisdom, establish it with understanding,
and through knowledge fill its rooms with
rare and beautiful treasure. Amen.*

*David's Prayer*
*of Repentance*

**Scripture Reading:** Psalm 51:1-19
**Key Verse:** Psalm 51:12 (NASB)

*Restore to me the joy of your salvation and*
*grant me a willing spirit, to sustain me.*

*I*n this psalm David pleads for forgiveness and cleansing (verses 1-2), confesses his guilt (verses 3-6), prays for pardon and restoration (verses 7-12), resolves to praise God (verses 13-17), and prays for the continued prosperity of Jerusalem (verses 18-19). This psalm elaborates David's confession of his sin with Bathsheba (2 Samuel chapters 11 and 12, with emphasis on 12:3).

This portion of Scripture highlights the highs of victory and the lows of defeat. We as sinners can appreciate how heavy David's heart was and his desire to approach his heavenly Father to ask forgiveness and to be restored in his daily walk of uprightness in the presence of God. The NIV translation of Psalm 51 reads so poetically that I thought you would like to read it with no interruptions.

Have mercy on me, O God, according to your unfailing love; according to your great compassion blot out my transgressions. Wash away all my iniquity and cleanse me from my sin.

For I know my transgressions, and my sin is always before me. Against you, you only, have I sinned and done what is evil in your sight, so that you are proved right when you speak and justified when you judge. Surely I was sinful at birth, sinful from the time my mother conceived me. Surely you desire truth in the inner parts; you teach me wisdom in the inmost place, Cleanse me with hyssop, and I will be clean; wash me, and I will be whiter than snow. Let me hear joy and gladness; let the bones you have crushed rejoice. Hide your face from my sins and blot out all my iniquity. Create in me a pure heart, O God, and renew a steadfast spirit within me. Do not cast me from your presence or take your Holy Spirit from me. Restore to me the joy of your salvation and grant me a willing spirit, to sustain me. Then I will teach transgressors your ways, and sinners will turn back to you.

Save me from bloodguilt, O God, the God

who saves me, and my tongue will sing of your righteousness.

O Lord, open my lips, and my mouth will declare your praise. You do not delight in sacrifice, or I would bring it; you do not take pleasure in burnt offerings.

The sacrifices of God are a broken spirit; a broken and contrite heart, O God, you will not despise.

In your good pleasure make Zion prosper; build up the walls of Jerusalem.

Then there will be righteous sacrifices, whole burnt offerings to delight you; then bulls will be offered on your altar.

This is a confession to meditate over. Chew it up and digest it. As I go over this confession, certain words and phrases touch my inner soul. Some of them include:

- Have mercy on me.
- Blot out my transgressions (sins).
- I have sinned against You.
- I have a sin nature since birth.
- Cleanse me and make me whiter than snow.
- Let me again hear joy and gladness.
- Blot out my iniquity.

- Create in me a pure heart.

- Renew a steadfast spirit within me.

- Don't cast me away.

- Restore my joy of Your salvation.

- Give me a willing spirit.

- I will teach others of Your ways.

- Save me from bloodguilt.

- My tongue will sing of Your righteousness.

- Open my lips and mouth for praise.

- Give me a broken and contrite heart.

As you examine this confession you see a man who has been broken and begs for restoration. I have never been to the depths of David's despair, but my sins have brought me to the place where I cry out to God, "Please forgive me, a helpless sinner."

First John 1:9 has been a great restoration promise for me. It reads, "If we confess our sins, He is faithful and righteous to forgive us our sins and to cleanse us from all unrighteousness."

Don't let the sun set on any unconfessed sin. Don't delay to confess because it will build up a callus around your heart and make repentance harder to deal with.

As I see and hear news stories that deal with crime, I see few people who confess and ask for forgiveness. They are always looking to find excuses:

- My father died when I was young.
- My home was very dysfunctional.
- My mother took drugs.
- My father drank a lot.
- I had a bad neighborhood.
- My schools were underfunded.

Excuse after excuse, but few people want to say as David did, "Against you, you only, have I sinned; please forgive me of my transgressions."

David realized that after confession there would be joy again. If you are burdened down today with a heavy heart because of unconfessed sin in your life, claim 1 John 1:9 and be restored to the joy of your salvation. God will create a pure heart within you.

*Father God, I want to give You all of my known and unknown sins today. I don't want to leave Your presence with any unconfessed sin in my life. I want to go away with a clean heart and have Your joy of forgiveness in me. Only by Your grace have You protected me from the ugliness of sin. Please be with the ladies who read today's psalm, so that they too will know of Your grace, love, and forgiveness. Amen.*

# Living by God's Surprises

**Scripture Reading:** James 1:2-12
**Key Verse:** James 1:2 (NASB)

*Consider it all joy, my brethren, when
you encounter various trials.*

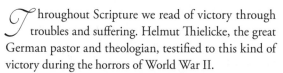

Throughout Scripture we read of victory through troubles and suffering. Helmut Thielicke, the great German pastor and theologian, testified to this kind of victory during the horrors of World War II.

When Thielicke said, "We live by God's surprises," he had personally suffered under the Nazis. As a pastor he wrote to young soldiers about to die; he comforted mothers and fathers and children after the bombs killed their loved ones. He preached magnificent sermons week after week as bombs blew apart his church and the lives and dreams of his parishioners. He spoke of God not only looking in love at His suffering people, weeping with them as they were surrounded by flames, but of God's hand reaching into the flames to help them, His own hand scorched by the fires.

From the depths of suffering and the wanton destruction during the Nazi regime, Thielicke held out a powerful Christian hope. To Germans disillusioned by the easily manipulated faith of their fathers, he quoted Peter Wust: "The great things happen to those who pray. But we learn to pray best in suffering."

Prayer, suffering, joy, and the surprises of God…they are all tightly enmeshed. But most shrink from the above statement, seeing suffering as the surest killer of both joy and "great things."

When we are rightly related to God, life is full of joyful uncertainty and expectancy…we do not know what God is going to do next; He packs our lives with surprises all the time.

What a strange idea: "joyful uncertainty." Most of us view uncertainty as cause for anxiety, not joy. Yet this call to expectancy rings true. The idea of standing on tiptoe to see what God is going to do next can transform our way of seeing. Prayers go maddeningly unanswered as well as marvelously fulfilled. Prayer becomes the lens through which we begin to see from God's perspective.[6]

When I read of men or women with such courage, I feel so insignificant when I approach God each day in prayer. It's hard for me to grasp the height of joy that these personalities of God must have experienced during this time in history. When James writes, "Consider it all joy, my brethren, when you encounter various trials, knowing that the testing of your faith produces endurance; and let endurance have its perfect result, that you may be perfect and complete, lacking in nothing" (James 1:2-4), I realize that life will be a challenge.

Who said that the Christian walk will be easy? These passages and events make me realize that there will be surprises when we live for God. We in America have it pretty easy compared to the rest of the world. Throughout Jesus' ministry He shared with His followers that there would be a cost if they followed Him.

Thielicke, along with the other historical pillars of the church, give testimony that prayer becomes the lens through which we begin to see life from God's perspective.

I hear many people ask in a harsh tone, "Well, I'm going to ask God when I get to heaven why He did...!" But I think we will stand in such awe in His presence that such questions will be meaningless, because then we will see history from God's point of view.

Wouldn't it be wonderful if when we got out of bed each morning we stood on our tiptoes to see what God is going to do today? We would joyfully look forward to see what God is going to do next. When we see life like that, our cup will surely "run over" and life will be joyful. Our cup will always be full, and as we pour out its contents God will give us new refreshment to fill it full again. Lord, I want to experience that joy!

*Father God, I want to live life so that I truly
live expectantly for Your surprises. I want to
tiptoe to see Your mysteries unveiled for me.
May I learn to see life from Your end, and forget
about all of man's wonderful knowledge, even
though it is magnificent. Give me depth in my
prayer life to match that of Helmut Thielicke.
Here is a man who undoubtedly saw Jesus face-
to-face with a true joy of assurance. Amen.*

# I Will Be with Your Mouth

**Scripture Reading:** Exodus 4:10-12
**Key Verse:** Exodus 4:12 (NASB)

*Now then go, and I, even I, will be with your
mouth, and teach you what you are to say.*

*B*ecause of the turmoil in my home as a child, I
decided I would not speak, in fear that I would
say the wrong thing. I became quiet and would grasp
my mother's leg in order to hide from people. I didn't
want to be around people; I was afraid of my own family
members and certainly strangers.

My father had a major drinking problem that put
everyone on pins and needles. Everyone watched what
he or she would say, because Daddy would get mad very
easily and make life miserable to the messenger who said
the wrong thing or in the wrong way.

I was this way until I got into high school and found
myself being liked by my fellow students. As a junior
I had the female lead in our senior play, "Best Foot

Forward." My success in this performance began to instill in me some self-confidence.

It was also at this time that I met my Bob, who made me feel safe to be around him and his loving family. But I was very quiet and reserved for fear that I might say the wrong thing. Bob would always say, "Emilie, speak up—you've got to tell me your thoughts on this," but I was very hesitant to express myself, fearing that I would say the wrong thing.

It wasn't until I was in my late twenties, when I signed up for a Christian women's retreat in Palm Springs, that I realized God had a speaking program for my life. Since the women of my church knew that I came from a Jewish faith, they asked me if I would give a three-minute testimony at the retreat. I felt like Moses in Exodus 4:10: "Please, Lord, I have never been eloquent, neither recently nor in time past, nor since Thou has spoken to thy servant; for I am slow of speech and slow of tongue." Then the Lord said to me as to Moses: "Who do you think made your mouth? Is it not I the Lord?"

So I reluctantly said, "Yes, I'll do it." I wasn't sure what I would say or how I would say it, but I had confidence that my Lord and God would be by my side.

Our key verse for today gave me great strength. God said to Moses: "Now then go, and I, even I, will be with your mouth, and teach you what you are to say." That was over 45 years ago, and He still goes before me, giving me the words to say and teaching me from His Word.

I can honestly say that God will be with your mouth. I travel all over this continent sharing with women of all denominations the words He has given me to say. Along with the spoken word, He has also entrusted me with writing more than 65 books, with well over five million books in print.

As a little girl who was afraid to speak I didn't have the faintest idea that God would use me to touch the lives of thousands through the spoken and written word. It only happened when God saw a willingness in my spirit to be used by Him.

My testimony was so well-received by those in the audience that I received many invitations to go to their local clubs to share my story. Of course, I had to expand it beyond the original three minutes to at least a 30-minute presentation, but God richly provided the words to say.

Am I still nervous when I get up to speak? Yes—every time. I still have to rely upon Him each time I speak to give me a peace and calm before I begin. I often wonder as I look out on the faces of my audience, "Why me, Lord? There are many better speakers and writers than I am." But He always answers back, "Now then go, and I will be with your mouth and teach you what to say."

*Father God, I am amazed that You have been*

able to use me—an ordinary wife, mother, and grandmother. You continue to amaze me in how You take the ordinary and make it extraordinary.

May I always be willing to share my story as long as there are people who want to hear it. The "bouquet of flowers" is laid at Your feet each night. You are to receive all the glory. Amen.

# Planning Your Days

**Scripture Reading:** Matthew 6:25-34
**Key Verse:** Matthew 6:33 (NASB)

*Seek first His kingdom and His righteousness,
and all these things shall be added to you.*

We live in a very anxious society. Many of us are more worried about tomorrow than today. We bypass all of today's contentment because of our worry about what might happen tomorrow. In our passage today we read that the early Christians asked the same basic questions (verse 31): What shall we eat? What shall we drink? With what shall we clothe ourselves?

Jesus tells them in verse 34, "Do not be anxious for tomorrow, for tomorrow will care for itself. Each day has enough trouble of its own." Then He gives them a formula for establishing the right priorities of life in verse 33: "Seek first His kingdom and His righteousness, and all these things shall be added to you." My Bob and I have used this verse as our mission verse for many years. Each day we claim these two instructions: Seek His kingdom and seek His righteousness.

When we seek these two things we find that our day takes shape and we can say "yes" we will do that or "no" we will not do that. Often we are overwhelmed by having too many things to do. Life offers many good choices on how to schedule our time. But we all have only 24 hours a day. How are we to use those hours effectively?

When we begin to set priorities, we determine what is important and what isn't, and how much time we are willing to give each activity.

The Bible gives us guidelines for the godly ordering of our lives:

- Our personal relationship to Him (Matthew 6:33; Philippians 3:8).
- Our time for home and family (Genesis 2:24; Psalm 127:3; 1 Timothy 3:2-5).
- Our time for work (1 Thessalonians 4:11-12).
- Our time for ministry and community activities (Colossians 3:17).

We cannot do all the things that come our way. My Bob and I have a saying that helps us when we have too many choices: "Say no to the good things and save each yes for the best."

Don't be afraid to say no. If you have established Matthew 6:33 as one of the key verses in your life you can very quickly decide whether a particular opportunity will help you to—seek God's kingdom; seek God's righteousness.

After learning to say no easily, you can begin to major on the big things of life and not get bogged down with issues that don't really matter.

*Father God, since You are a God of order I also want to have order in my life. Thank You for sharing this verse with our family many years ago. It has certainly helped us to major on the major and minor on the minor issues of life. May other women get excited about not being anxious for tomorrow and realize that You take care of our daily needs. Amen.*

# The Blankie

**Scripture Reading:** John 14:27-31
**Key Verse:** John 14:27 (NASB)

*Peace I leave with you; My peace I give to you.
Not as the world gives do I give to you. Let not
your heart be troubled, nor let it be fearful.*

When our first grandchild was born, her parents named her Christine Marie—Christine from her mother's middle name and Marie from my middle name. As a namesake I'm very proud of Christine Marie. At this writing she is our only granddaughter, along with four grandsons. We love them too!

From flannel fabric I made her a piece of pink-printed blanket with some small roses. The blanket was edged with a pink satin binding. It was only about 8 inches square. Well, as you might guess, it became her security blankie while she sucked her thumb. The blankie got twisted, wadded up, and smoothed by little Christine. She was finally able to pull loose an end and twist the threads around her fingers.

Christine loved her pink rosebud blankie. It gave her

comfort when she was hurt, softness when she was afraid, and security when she felt alone. Then one day five years later the blankie got folded one last time and was put in an envelope that she tucked away in her dresser drawer.

When Christine was 13, from time to time she would pull out that envelope to look at the rosebud flannel security blanket.

Jesus is like the security blanket that Christine once held close to her—only today she has almighty God our heavenly Father, God the Son, and God the Holy Spirit to hold tight to.

As our Scripture states, Jesus is who gives us peace in the midst of the storms of life: when we are going through that difficult tornado of a broken marriage, the death of a dream, financial troubles, childless pain, ill health, or all the other trials we encounter in just living out our daily lives.

Christ is our security blanket when we are afraid and feel fearful of tomorrow. My mama used to tell me in the middle of the night when I needed to go to the bathroom but was afraid of the dark, "Be afraid, but go." Today I know I can go because I have my Lord, who is with me wherever I go. When I'm weak and upset, He holds me and comforts my heart.

Jesus is much more than a security blanket. He is our Comforter, our Savior, the Messiah, the Alpha and Omega, the Almighty, our bright and morning star, our counselor, our strength, our redeemer, our peace, our high priest, our foundation, and our master builder.

First Corinthians 3:11 says, "No man can lay a foundation other than the one which is laid, which is Jesus Christ."

It's time to give our blanket over to Jesus and allow Him to be our Master Comforter.

Christine's blankie is now in a beautiful frame, hanging on the wall in her bedroom as a treasured memory of her babyhood. She will carry this along her lifetime from babyhood into her golden years. But best of all, she will carry Jesus in her heart for eternity.

*Father God, thank You for letting me put away
my old childhood security blanket and giving
me the faith to trust You in all situations.
May I never go back to my blankie. You have
been so faithful to me during these adult years.
You are all I need—nothing else. Amen.*

# You Are Not Alone

**Scripture Reading:** Matthew 6:1-13
**Key Verse:** Matthew 6:9-13 (The Lord's Prayer)

*This, then, is how you should pray:*
*"Our Father in heaven, hallowed be your name..."*

Some of you may not have a prayer life at all. Others of you may have a very vital prayer life. Some of you want to have a prayer life but are fumbling with it because you don't know how to incorporate it into your life or how to organize it. I was once in that position. I was fumbling in my prayer life because I didn't know the steps to take. One of my first learnings was to trust God for my every care. Often in life I had been disappointed by those I trusted, but the following helped me realize I was never alone.

## One Set of Footprints

One night a man had a dream. In his dream he was walking along the beach with the Lord, when across the sky flashed all the events of his life. However, for each scene he noticed two sets of footprints in the sand, one belonging to him and the other to the Lord. When the last scene had flashed before him, he looked back at the footprints and noticed that many times along the path there was only one set of footprints in the sand. He also noticed that this happened during the lowest and saddest times of his life.

This really bothered him, so he said to the Lord, "You promised that once I decided to follow You, You would walk with me all the way, but I noticed that during the roughest times of my life there was only one set of footprints. I don't understand why You deserted me when I needed You the most."

The Lord replied, "My precious child, I love you and I would never leave you. During those times of trial and suffering when you saw only one set of footprints, it was then that I carried you."

—Author Unknown

You see, God is always with us. When the times are the lowest, that's when He picks us up and carries us. Isn't that wonderful! Some of us right now are in a position where we're being carried through a rough situation or problem in our life. It's wonderful to know that we have our Lord there to carry us when times get low and things get rough.

Often we don't take the necessary time with our Lord in prayer and communication. But do you know what? He loves us anyway. He loves us unconditionally. Prayer doesn't have to be long, either. Sometimes we get turned off because we feel it takes so much time, but it doesn't have to be long.

In several of my books I have given you a way in which you can organize your daily prayer life so you aren't overwhelmed with this phase of your spiritual life. Please refer to those chapters for a step-by-step plan for an organized prayer life. As I introduce ladies to prayer who aren't accustomed to a disciplined life of prayer, I want them first to be exposed to the model prayer as found in today's readings. The Lord's Prayer—

- begins with adoration of God (verse 9);
- acknowledges subjection to His will (verse 10);
- asks petitions of Him (verses 11-13a);
- ends with praise (verse 13b).

To better understand this prayer, we break it down into small phrases with their meanings. This gives us a model for all our prayers (NASB):

- *"Our Father who art in heaven"* (verse 9a). Recognize who He is—the Person of God.
- *"Hallowed be Thy name"* (verse 9b). Worship God because of who He is.

- *"Thy kingdom come. Thy will be done"* (verse 10). Seek and do God's will. His Word is the way to find His will.

- *"Give us this day our daily bread"* (verse 11). Ask God to meet your everyday needs in order to perform your godly work.

- *"And forgive us our debts"* (verse 12). Ask God for pardon and forgiveness in your daily failures.

- *"And do not lead us into temptation"* (verse 13). Ask for protection from the evils of temptation.

- *"For Thine is the kingdom and the power and the glory"* (verse 13). Praise God for who He is.

*Father God, I so appreciate the Lord's Prayer. So many times in life I am able to recite it in moments of need and praise. I thank You for being my heavenly Father. Since my earthly father lacked some parenting skills that a young daughter needed, I find You a great support and encouragement for me in time of need. With You I find I am never alone. Amen.*

# A Moment of Grace

**Scripture Reading:** Ephesians 2:1-9
**Key Verse:** Ephesians 2:8-9 (NASB)

*By grace you have been saved, through faith; and
that not of yourselves, it is the gift of God; not as
a result of works, that no one should boast.*

*I*n the following story we can see the power of grace
at work...

During my senior year in high school I had been sick
with bronchitis and missed two weeks of school. When I
returned I had to make up nine tests in one week. By the
last one I was really out of it. I remember looking at this
test paper and not knowing any of the answers. I was a
total blank. It was like I had never heard of this history
junk before.

It was after school and I was the only one in the
classroom. The teacher was working at his desk and I
was staring off into space. "What's the matter?" he asked.
And I said, "I can't do this. I don't know any of these
answers." He got up and came over and looked at my
paper and said, "You know the answer to that! We just

talked about it in class yesterday. You answered a question I asked about that." I said, "I don't remember. I just can't remember." He gave me a few hints, but I still couldn't remember. I realized that I was on overload, and my straight A's in history were now a thing of the past. I looked at him and I said,

"Look. You're just gonna have to give me an F. I can't do it. I feel too bad." He reached down with his red pencil and I watched him, certain he was going to put an F on my paper—I mean, there was not one answer on this test! But he put an A on the top.

I said, "What are you doing?" And he said, "If you'd been here and you felt good and you'd had time to study, that's what you'd have gotten. So that's what you're gonna get." This guy really did recognize that I had been operating out of excellence all the time I had been in his class, and that I was telling the truth. My mind was a blank and I was willing to take the F, because that's what I deserved. But I didn't have to.

I then realized that there are people out there who will give you a break once in a while. It was empowering. It was like he was saying, "I know who you are, not just what you do." That's an amazing gift to give somebody. I will be grateful to that guy till the day I die. I thought, "That's the kind of teacher I want to be."[7]

What an excellent example of how God has given us, undeserving sinners, salvation and immediate acceptance by Him through what His Son did on the cross for us.

We are saved through faith in Jesus. This faith involves knowledge of the gospel (Romans 10:14), acknowledgment of the truth of its message, and personal reception of the Savior (John 1:12). Paul states that works cannot save (Ephesians 2:9), but that good works should always accompany salvation (James 2:17).

Even though we cannot make a complete biblical comparison from a story such as today's, we do find a teacher who bestowed grace on his pupil.

By all rights the student deserved an F on his grade, but the teacher was willing to give him an A because of who he was. The teacher knew the pupil's heart and his efforts of the past.

This is where we are in life without Christ. We deserve an F grade because we, in ourselves, are sinners and do not deserve anything more. However, Jesus went to the cross for us and died for our sins, so that by faith we would accept His act for us personally. Through God's grace, and His grace alone, and His grace only, our grade went from an F to an A because of our faith in God's Son, Jesus. The cross of Christ divides every other religion from Christianity. That's why the events surrounding the cross are paramount to us as Christians.

*Father God, I come to You humbly in prayer,*
*thanking You for Your grace upon my life. I*

would not want to go around for the rest of my life with an F stamped on me. There would be no hope in this world. Maybe that's why I see so many sad people. They have never received Your grace and have never gone from darkness to light. Thank You, thank You for my salvation through Your undeserved grace to me! Amen.

*A Prayer for
All Seasons*

**Scripture Reading:** Colossians 1:9-12
**Key Verse:** Colossians 1:9

*Since the day we heard about you, we have
not stopped praying for you and asking God to
fill you with the knowledge of his will through
all spiritual wisdom and understanding.*

Time has a way of defining true friends. I have discovered that passing years and growing distance are ineffective obstacles to the mutual love between my friends and me. Perhaps it is because of our common walk with the Lord that we can just pick up where we left off whenever we are together. And these are the dear ones I will spend eternity loving!

Of course, prayer is an important part of continuing that bond. Colossians 1:3-14 is an eloquent description of a Christian's prayer for her friends. Even though Paul had not even visited the Christians at Colosse (Colossians 1:7), his love for them through Christ was strong and ardent.[8]

139

As we spend time with God, we open ourselves to His work in our hearts and in our lives. Then, as we see Him working, we will want to know Him even more. We will want our prayer life to be all that it can be. What does that mean? How should we be praying?

In the Scripture, we find many models of prayer, and probably foremost is the Lord's Prayer (Matthew 6:9-13). This wonderful example of a prayer includes important elements of prayer. We find words of adoration, of submission to God's will, of petition, and in closing, of praise. We can learn much from the model our Lord gave when His disciples said, "Teach us to pray" (Luke 11:1).

As meaningful as the Lord's Prayer is to me, I have also found Colossians 1:9-12 to be a powerful guide in my prayer life. If you aren't in the habit of praying or if you want to renew your time with God, I challenge you to read this passage of Scripture every day for 30 days. Look at it in small pieces, dwell on its message each day, take action upon what it says, and you'll become a new person.

Read today's Scripture passage again and think about what a wonderful prayer it is for you to pray for your friend. Knowing that a friend is praying for me is a real source of encouragement and support. If you aren't praying for your friends daily, let me suggest that Colossians 1:9-12 be your model. Look at what you'll be asking God:

- That your friend will have the spiritual wisdom and understanding she needs to know God's will.

- That she will "walk in a manner worthy of the Lord, to please him, in all respects" (verse 10).

- That your friend will be bearing "fruit in all good work and increasing in the knowledge of God" (verse 10).

- That she will be "strengthened with all power... for the attaining of all steadfastness and patience" (verse 11).

- You would then end your prayer by joyously giving thanks to God for all that He has given you—your friend being one of those gifts (verse 12).

Did you hear those words? What an armor of protection and growth you can give your friend with a prayer like that! With these powerful words and the Lord at her side, your friend will be able to deal with the challenges she faces. I also encourage you to tell your friend that you are praying for her each day, and if she is receptive, tell her the specifics of your prayers for her. Let me assure you that it is a real comfort to have a friend praying for me, asking God to give me wisdom and understanding, to enable me to honor Him in all I do, to help me bear fruit for His kingdom, and to grant me strength, steadfastness, and patience.

Know, too, that these verses from Colossians are a good model for your prayers for your husband, other members of your family, your neighbors, and yourself.

After all, all of God's people need to know His will, honor Him in everything they do, grow in the knowledge of the Lord, and be strong, steadfast, and patient as we serve Him.

*Father God, there's nothing like a praying friend. I thank You for giving me so many. In turn may I reach out and support each of them in their time of need. Amen.*

# Becoming as Gold

**Scripture Reading:** Job 23:1-12
**Key Verse:** Job 23:10

*But he knows the way that I take; when he
has tested me, I will come forth as gold.*

When pain comes into our lives it's so easy to ask "Why, Lord? Why, Lord, do the righteous suffer?"

If there ever was a man who loved and obeyed God, it was Job. Yet his testing was very dramatic and ever so painful. Today all we have to do is pick up a newspaper in any part of the world and we can read of tragedy touching the just and the unjust.

Our friends Glen and Marilyn Heavilin have lost three sons prematurely: one to crib death, one twin, Ethan, to pneumonia as an infant, then the second twin, Nathan, was killed as a teenager by a drunk driver. Were Glen and Marilyn tested? You bet. Yet did they come forth as gold? You bet! Today they use their experiences to glorify the name of the Lord.

Marilyn has written five books. Her first, *Roses in*

*December,*[9] tells the story of their great loss. Marilyn has had the opportunity to speak all over the country in high school auditoriums filled with teenagers. There she shares her story and has the platform to talk about life and death, chemical dependency, and God Himself.

Did God know what He was doing when He chose the Heavilins? You bet. They have come forth as gold fired in the heat of life and polished to shine for Him. Is their pain gone? Never. Can they go forth to minister? Absolutely. They have been very active in a group called "Compassionate Friends" which supports families who have experienced the death of a child. I thank God for Christians like the Heavilins. God knew the way they would take when tragedy came into their lives.

Everyone has experienced some kind of tragedy. How we handle these events when they happen is key. Today there are so many wonderful support groups available in churches and the local communities.

I grew up with a violent, alcoholic father. I had no place to go and no one to talk to, so I stuffed my pain. Now there are several groups to help people who find themselves in situations like mine.

A church in Southern California has a large group that meets weekly and has become like a church within a church for those who are chemically dependent and for their families. Lives have changed as they pray for each other, support each other, and cry together. Many are coming forth as gold.

Bob and I visited a church in Memphis, Tennessee, which had a support group for homosexuals. Because of this church's outreach, many were coming out of the gay lifestyle and coming forth as gold.

Whatever your test is today, please know that others have experienced and are experiencing your pain. Don't go through the testing alone. Contact the local church and find another with whom you can share and cry. You, too, can and will come forth as gold.

Jesus knows and has also experienced our pain. He is always with us to help us get through the tough times in life. Trust Him now. It's all part of the coming forth as gold that Job talks about.

*Father God, it is hard to desire testing in order*
*to be more Christlike. However, I know from*
*experience that we rarely grow in good times.*
*It's the intense heat that makes us pure. May I*
*be gold and not wood, hay, or stubble. Amen.*

# A House Divided

**Scripture Reading:** Mark 3:24-27
**Key Verse:** Mark 3:5

*If a house is divided against itself, that house cannot stand.*

"A house divided against itself cannot stand," Abraham Lincoln said in his acceptance speech of his nomination for the United States Senate. "Either the opponents of slavery will arrest the further spread of it and place it where the public mind shall rest in the belief that it is in the course of ultimate extinction, or its advocates will push it forward, till it shall become alike lawful in all the states, old as well as new—north as well as south."

Lincoln's pursuit of the equality of peoples eventually brought his defeat in the Senate election. Lincoln responded to his downfall philosophically: "…and though I now sink out of view and shall be forgotten, I believe I have made some marks which will tell for the cause of civil liberty long after I am gone." Lincoln certainly didn't "sink out of view"! He left marks not only upon our country but on the whole world. His gift to the United States was to heal those hurts that wanted to divide us, to bring together those who had been at war.

Many of our families are divided and need to be healed and brought together. I had two aunts (they were sisters) who hadn't spoken to each other for 10 years because of some insignificant verbal disagreement. They behaved like little children with small hurts who could not let their souls confess their error. As I saw my aunts get older without sharing their later years in harmony, I decided that I was going to be the peacemaker, even though I was 30-plus years younger than they were. I was able to arrange a family gathering where both attended. After a short time together in this setting, they began to open up and talk to each other. By the end of the evening they had made amends. Because of this reuniting, they were able to enjoy the last 15 years of their lives together as sisters.

Maybe you have division in your family. As today's Scripture reading states, "If a kingdom is divided against itself, that kingdom cannot stand." If we stay divided we know what the outcome will be—collapse of the family unit. *You* become the healer of your divided home. It will take much prayer, patience, and conviction, but in the end you'll discover that a united house has many blessings.

By wisdom a house is built, and through understanding it is established; through knowledge its
rooms are filled with rare and beautiful treasures.

PROVERBS 24:3-4

You be the one to restore your house with a rare and
beautiful spirit.

*Father God, may I be a healer in my family.
May my spirit be one that unifies rather than
divides. Show me any traits that I might
have that need change. I thank You for being
here when I need You. Thank You for Your
continuing love and Your sweet spirit. Amen.*

# The Whys of Life

**Scripture Reading:** Ecclesiastes 7:13-18
**Key Verse:** Ecclesiastes 7:16

*Do not be overrighteous, neither be
overwise—why destroy yourself?*

*Y*ou and I know that fame is fleeting. I always had
my parents to refresh my memory.

No matter how important you think you are, they
taught me, you're a mere nothing in the passage of time.
Once you reach a certain level in a material way, what
more can you do? You can't eat more than three meals
a day; you'll kill yourself. You can't wear two suits, one
over the other. You might now have three cars in your
garage—but six! Oh, you can indulge yourself, but only
to a point.

One way to make sure fame doesn't change you is to
keep in mind that you're allotted only so much time on
this earth—and neither money nor celebrity will buy you
a couple of extra days. Although I do have a rich friend
in New York who says, "What do you mean I can't take

it with me? I've already made out traveler's checks and sent them ahead."

Life is so complicated that it's hard for anyone, especially kids, to figure out what their purpose is in life, and to whom they're accountable. Of course, we should all be accountable to God throughout our lives—and live our lives that way every day, not just on our deathbeds begging for forgiveness.

A lot of people don't believe in God because they can't see Him. I'm not a Doubting Thomas, though. I truly believe. When we were kids, our Hebrew school teachers used to address this question by telling us: "You can't see electricity either, but it's there. Just stick your hand in the socket now and then to remind yourself." I've never seen an ozone layer or carbon monoxide or an AIDS virus, but they're out there somewhere.[10]

Lee Iacocca has learned a very valuable lesson in life, and that is balance and proper perspective toward wealth and fame. The wise man will live life in obedience to God, recognizing that God will eventually judge all men.

In today's Scripture reading we see that God brings both prosperity and adversity into our lives for His sovereign purpose without always revealing His plan. Our minds do not have the horsepower to think as God does. By faith we must rely on His words to do what He says He will do. A long time ago Bob and I claimed 2 Timothy 3:16-17 as one of our important verses of

Scripture, "All Scripture is God-breathed and is useful for teaching, rebuking, correcting and training in righteousness, so that the man of God may be thoroughly equipped for every good work."

Are you being equipped to handle life: birth, death, fame, divorce, fortune, bankruptcy, health, sickness? When we're young we often think we know all the answers of life. But as we get older we begin to realize that we fit into a master plan that can't always be explained.

Have you ever asked the question, "Why?" Of course you have. We all have. That is the mystery question of life. Solomon realized that God has a sovereign purpose, and that He doesn't always reveal to us the key to His plan.

*Father God, humble my spirit so that I might be open to new truths today that I might better understand the whys of life (the big and the small). You know that I want to expand my mind to be more like You! Amen.*

# His
# Outstretched Hand

**Scripture Reading:** Isaiah 53:3-10

**Key Verse:** Isaiah 53:3a

*He was despised and rejected by men, a man
of sorrows and familiar with suffering.*

$\mathcal{R}$ ejection can hurt so bad that you think you want to
die. We all have experienced it from time to time,
probably from someone we cared about very deeply—a
parent, husband, child, friend, brother or sister, or possibly all the above.

What great pain this can cause, and yet we can
overcome the pain of rejection. Yes, there is life after
rejection.

Jesus Himself experienced rejection. If anyone knows
this pain, it's Jesus. His own people who He came to save
and teach were the very ones who nailed Him to the
cross: "He came to that which was his own, but his own
did not receive him" (John 1:11).

My Jewish family wanted me to marry within my

own faith. Yet when I was 16, my Bob introduced me to Christ. Within a few months Bob and I were engaged, and eight months later we were married. My very own family, those I loved, rejected me for my stand with Jesus and my stand to marry the Christian young man I loved.

God honored my heart and my faithfulness to Him. My family grew to adore my Bob as I do, and our family was restored.

It didn't happen all at once, but in His time, one by one, hearts were softened and attitudes changed. The pain in my heart was great, but little by little His mighty strength took over and peace filled my heart. I hung in and loved my family when it was difficult to love the attitudes and mockery thrown at me. I'm grateful today I trusted Jesus.

Isaiah prophesied that Messiah would be despised and rejected of men, yet this foreknowledge did not make the experience any less painful for Jesus. And to make it even worse, Jesus felt rejected by His own Father. When Jesus bore the sins of the world He felt deep, deep pain. He cried out, "My God, my God, why have you forsaken me?" (Matthew 27:46).

Yet in the middle of all this rejection, Jesus never abandoned the mission that God had given to Him. He never fought back against the ones who rejected Him. How did He respond? With love—love even for those who crucified Him.

Do you think the Lord knows how you feel? You bet! And the Lord Jesus offers you His strength. The Bible says that He sympathizes with our weakness and He offers His grace for our time of need. When Jesus suffered on the cross, He bore our penalty for us. He paid the price for our sins. Then He gave us a promise: "Never will I leave you; never will I forsake you" (Hebrews 13:5). No matter what happens, God will never reject you. You will never be alone again. You may be rejected by others, but remember God Almighty will always be there to comfort you. His hand is stretched out to you. All you need to do is place your hands in His. Allow His strength to empower you today.

*Father God, You know rejection far better than
I do. I ask You to touch me when I'm rejected (or
when I feel rejected) and ease that pain. Please
make me sensitive to the times when I reject
people. You know that I don't want to hurt others'
feelings. Protect my words, body language, and
attitude, that they may heal and not reject. Amen.*

*Your True Motivation*

**Scripture Reading:** Matthew 19:27–20:16

**Key Verse:** Matthew 19:29

*And everyone who has left houses or brothers
or sisters or father or mother or children or
fields for my sake will receive a hundred times
as much and will inherit eternal life.*

Throughout my life I have asked myself over and over, why do I serve? What is my motivation for speaking, writing, giving financially to the church, being a mother, giving freely to my husband and to my extended family?

In today's passage Peter asks Jesus, "What then will there be for us?" Have you ever caught yourself asking this very basic question? I know I have. When Bob was in business, he would share with me the reaction from different employees when he would tell them about a promotion they were going to receive. Most would ask:

- How much more money will I make?

- Any increase in health insurance, vacations, bonuses, retirement, etc?

In the verses you read, Jesus answers Peter's very basic question, giving us three important principles for our daily living:

- Whatever we give up we will receive a hundred times as much.

- We will inherit eternal life.

- Many who are first will be last, and many who are last will be first.

Many times in our religious life we think God will punish us if we don't serve Him rather than being truly motivated by a pure desire to serve Him.

My daily prayer is for God to reveal to me what my true motivation is in serving Him. In Psalm 139:1 David states, "O LORD, you have searched me and you know me." I truly yearn to know me as God knows me.

Can I accept from God the promises He has given me in today's beautiful reading? Do we honestly accept by faith what God has so graciously given to us, a hundredfold return for all we have given up *and* eternal life because of our acceptance of Jesus?

As I look around to see what God has so graciously given to me, I am amazed and blessed at His generosity. As the old church hymn says, "Count your blessings, name them one by one." Name a few:

- I know Jesus face-to-face
- salvation
- family
- a wonderful home
- a wonderful ministry
- improved health
- a Bible-teaching church

The third principle, that the last shall be first, I found puzzling. But I was looking at it through man's eyes, rather than taking time to see what God was trying to teach me. We all want to be fair in our dealings with other people and in their dealings with us, yet this passage seemed unfair. Why would the farmer pay the late worker the same amount as the early worker who had been in the fields all day?

In Matthew 20:14 the owner of the farm says, "I want to give the man who was hired last the same as I gave you." To me this represents God's amazing grace and generosity that knows no bounds. What we as women might feel is right is irrelevant. God chooses to do what He chooses to do.

Are we willing to serve God? Our reward is eternal life—even if we come to the field at three o'clock in the afternoon and others have been there since early morning.

*Father God, search my heart and test my motivation for what I do. Don't let any selfishness enter into my life. You know my intent. May my actions be done with a clear heart. Amen.*

*In all your ways acknow*
*he will make your path*

Do you have the type of home where nothin
to get done? Where each room would take a
dozer just to clean up the mess? You rush around all
never completing any one job, or if you do complete a
task, there is a little one behind you, pulling and messing
everything up again! There isn't one of us who *hasn't*
experienced these feelings.

When I was 20 our baby daughter Jennifer was six
months old. We then took in my brother's three children and within a few months I became pregnant. That
gave Bob and me five children under five years old. My
life was work, work, work—and yet I never seemed to
get anywhere. I was running on a treadmill that never
stopped and never moved ahead. I was always tired and
never seemed to get enough done, let alone get enough
sleep. I was fragmented, totally confused, and stressed.

*Overload*

ading: Proverbs 3:1-8

Proverbs 3:6

*...ledge him, and*
*...straight.*

*...g seems*
*bull-*
*...ay*

...ner

...d my Lord and I

...d and prayed.

...committed 15 minutes each day to the organization of our home, concentrating on things I never seemed to get done: the silverware drawer, refrigerator, hall closets, photos, bookshelves, piles of papers. I committed to this for 30 days and the pattern was set. God was directing my path. Our home changed dramatically. The cloud of homemaking stress lifted, and I had new direction. The Lord redeemed my time with Him. I had more time to plan meals, make new recipes, play with the children, take walks to the park, even catch a nap from time to time.

# Spread the Fragrance

**Scripture Reading:** 2 Corinthians 2:14-17
**Key Verse:** 2 Corinthians 2:14

*But thanks be to God who always leads us in triumphal procession in Christ and through us spreads everywhere the fragrance of the knowledge of Him.*

The dictionary defines "fragrant" as a pleasant odor. The opposite of that would be the smell of a baby's dirty diaper! Yet how sweet the smell of a clean, freshly lotioned and powdered baby after his bath. Baby and mother are happy as the sweet smell permeates the nursery. One baby, two different smells. One you want to hand over to Mom as quickly as you can and the other you want to reach out and pick up from Mom's arms.

Today's Scripture reading says that as we grow in the knowledge of Jesus Christ we become a sweet odor to others. We become a fragrance others want to enjoy and hang around with.

In California, where we lived for 33 years, the orange blossoms in the spring from our orange trees became so potent that the aroma permeated the entire area. The evenings were beautiful with the smell. We kept the bedroom French doors open just to enjoy the fragrance. After a while the blossoms died away and tiny green oranges appeared. They slowly grew, and in the late fall those green oranges turned to orange. In December we began to pick, eat, juice, and give away. But it isn't until late-January, mid-February, that the sugar content is at its height. That's when the fresh orange juice is oh-so-sweet and wonderful. But we never forget the fragrance of the first blooms. Does the fragrance die? Not at all. The smell of that sweet juice is just as wonderful as the blossom.

What is your fragrance? Are you one who others don't want to be around? Or are others wanting to smell the freshness of your sweet spirit because you are a blossom so strong with the fragrance of the spirit of Christ? It takes the knowledge of God's Word to develop that fragrance—learning about God's holy book and the principles taught chapter by chapter.

Where do we begin? We begin with the tiny bloom of time in God's Word, the Bible. A little now, a little later, step-by-step as the months go by we begin to mature just like the orange. We become so full of God's juices that others want to pick us up and squeeze His fragrance from us. The sweetness gets even sweeter as we share His Word with others, pouring out what we've filled our juice pitcher with. As His fragrance enters others' lives, they then begin the same process—a small blossom growing to full maturity. As the process continues from person to person, our orange tree will be full of blossoms, creating a fragrance that can eventually permeate the whole city and eventually the world.

*Father God, may those around me smell the sweet fragrance of Jesus. May it be so attractive that they draw close to You. Amen.*

# Find Favor in God's Eyes

**Scripture Reading:** Genesis 6:8-22
**Key Verse:** Genesis 6:8,22

*Noah found favor in the eyes of the LORD.... Noah did everything just as God commanded him.*

Almost every day we can read newspaper articles dealing with people who are being honored by the world:

- government
- sports
- medicine
- education
- theater
- music

On and on we can go. Man finding favor with man. Have you ever thought how much richer it would be to have God find favor with you? I stand in awe when I think of God finding favor in me, but He does. Only through His marvelous grace are we able to come to Him face-to-face.

Noah lived in a world much like today, a world full of sin. Man hasn't changed much over the centuries—we just give sin a different name. Yet through all this wickedness, Noah was a person who lived a godly life. His life was pleasing to God even during those evil days.

Noah didn't find favor because of his individual goodness but through his personal faith in God. We are also judged according to the same standard—that of our personal faith and obedience. My daily prayer is that my family and I will be worthy of the goodness God so richly bestows upon us.

Even though Noah was upright and blameless before God, he wasn't perfect. God recognized that Noah's life reflected a *genuine* faith, not always a *perfect* faith. Do we sometimes feel all alone in our walk with God? Noah walked in greater deprivation than we, yet he still walked with God (verse 9). Noah found that it wasn't the surroundings of his life that kept him in close fellowship with God, but it was the heart of Noah that qualified him to find friendship with God.

How often do we try to find favor with man only to fall on our face in rejection? Noah only wanted to please God. Have you ever asked in that small voice of yours, "Do I find favor in the eyes of the Lord?" When we come to Him and admit we are sinners, we please God. At that time we find God's grace, and we are able to move into a relationship with Jesus Christ. Then we are able to find favor with God.

As we live in this very difficult time of world history, we might ask, "Do I find favor in God's sight?" God gives us grace to live victoriously: "He gives us more grace" (James 4:6).

*Father God, oh may I find favor with You. What an honor for Noah to be favored by You, yet I realize that he was obedient to Your Word. Give me a hunger to fall in love with Your Word and put it to work in my life. You are worthy of praise. Amen.*

# *His Name Is Wonderful*

**Scripture Reading:** Isaiah 9:6-7

**Key Verse:** Isaiah 9:6b

*And he will be called Wonderful Counselor, Mighty God, Everlasting Father, Prince of Peace.*

His name is Wonderful, Jesus my Lord. His name is full of wonder, miracles, excitement, fulfillment, peace, and joy. There is something about that name! Our thoughts today must be positive—looking for the good and wonderfulness of the Lord. He is Almighty God who parted the Red Sea, raised Lazarus from the dead, and lives today in our hearts, wanting to be a miracle in our lives.

As Isaiah wrote, "Of the increase of his government or peace there will be no end."

The peace of Jesus is in our hearts. God didn't promise joy, but He did say He would increase our peace.

To be sure, life will bring sorrow, broken hearts,

health problems, financial difficulties, and much, much more. Our life in and with our Lord will bring dependence, maturity, refreshment, refuge, redemption, righteous judgment, and many rewards. Plus, He will restore your heart, mind, and soul.

Take your problems and worries of today, wrap them in a box, and close the lid very tightly. Then, my dear, put it into the wonderful hands of Jesus. Now walk away and don't take it back. Eighty percent of the things we worry about never happen anyway—so let Jesus take the remaining 20 percent. He will give back to you 100 percent of His life and peace. In fact, He has done it already for you as He hung on the cross of Calvary.

Let's sing His wonderful name: Jesus, Jesus, Jesus. There is just something about that name!

*Father God, You have so many wonderful
names. May I search out the Scripture and
really get to know You by Your names.
Each one has a special meaning and gives
me deeper understanding to who You are.
Reveal Your character to me today. Amen.*

# I'm Special Because

**Scripture Reading:** Psalm 139:13-17
**Key Verse:** Psalm 139:14

*I praise you because I am fearfully and wonderfully made; your works are wonderful, I know that full well.*

One evening our seven-year-old grandson, Chad, was helping me set the dinner table. Whenever the grandchildren come over, we have a tradition of honoring someone at the table with our red plate that says, "You Are Special Today" (even though it isn't a birthday, anniversary, or other special occasion). It was natural for me to ask Chad, "Who should we honor today with our special plate?" Chad said, "How about *me?*" "Yes, Chad, you are special," I replied. "It's your day."

He was so proud as we all sat around the table and said our blessing. Then Chad said, "I think it would be very nice if everyone around the table would tell me why they think I'm special." Bob and I got a chuckle out of that, but we thought it might be a good idea, so we did it. After we were all through Chad said, "Now I want to tell you why I think I'm special. I'm special because I'm a child of God." Chad was so right on. Psalm 139:13-14 tells us that God knew us before we were born. He knit us together in our mother's womb and we are wonderfully made.

When I was seven, 10, or even 22, I could not have told anyone why I was special. I didn't even talk, I was so shy. My alcoholic father would go into a rage, swearing and throwing things. I was afraid I'd say the wrong thing, so I didn't talk. My self-image wasn't too good. But the day came when I read Psalm 139, and my heart came alive with the realization that I, too, am special because I am a child of God. And so are you. We were uniquely made as He knit us together in our mother's womb.

Verse 16 says, "All the days are ordained for me." It's not by accident you are reading this devotion today. Perhaps you, too, need to know how very special you are. We have all been given unique qualities, talents, and gifts. And you, my dear one, have been made by God. You are His child. He loves you more than any earthly father could possibly love you. Because He is your heavenly Father, Almighty God, He cares for you even when you don't care for yourself. You are His child even when you feel far from Him. It's never your heavenly Father who moves away from you. It's you who moves away from Him.

Today is ordained by God for you to draw near to Him and allow Him to be near to you. Because today is your day, my friend, "You Are Special Today." A child of God, as Chad said.

*Father God, thank You for making me so special, with a heart to love You more and more each day. Please today help me to draw near to You and to feel Your presence. Thank You for being my heavenly Father. I know that I'm never alone. You are always with me. Amen.*

# The Quiet Spirit

**Scripture Reading:** 1 Peter 3:1-9
**Key Verse:** 1 Peter 3:4

*Instead, it should be that of your inner self, the unfading beauty of a gentle and quiet spirit, which is of great worth in God's sight.*

It's been a tough day. You were late getting off work, the children need picking up at day care, you have no clue as to what to have for dinner, and the car needs gas. Stopping at the market to pick up some kind of food is a disaster—the checkout lines are long and the checkers are slow. Finally you get home, kick off the shoes from your aching feet, and throw the food on the stove, turning it up high to cook faster for starving and cranky children. The phone rings and the dog barks while the children cry for dinner. Are you supposed to have a quiet and gentle spirit? You probably don't even want one.

You know what I used to do on days like that? I would go into the bathroom, stick my head in the toilet, and cry to God, "If You only knew what it's like out there, You wouldn't let me be in this situation." Sometimes I would have to make two or three trips in and out of the bathroom until I could settle down enough to say, "Lord, help me!" I would then count to 10, take a deep breath, and attack.

You know how you can avoid days like this? By making a plan for just those kind of days! Plan ahead by preparing make-ahead freezer meals, getting gas in the car before it reaches empty, and having on hand a quick, pre-dinner snack for the children—pretzels, popcorn, a few crackers and cheese, or a frozen smoothie.

It's not God who gives the confusion. It's our own mismanagement of time and organization.

The quiet spirit comes as we plan to eliminate the stress in our life. We must learn to slow down and refocus our goals and priorities.

There was a woman in my Bible study who had 10 children. Jeanette was worn out physically. She needed dental work and a good haircut. Her clothes didn't fit, and her shoes were worn over on the heels. Yet she came to the study every week by bus, and she was always prepared. She added great spiritual depth to the class. This busy, overworked mother had a beautiful inner spirit, and after our first study together, none of us saw the outside of Jeanette. We saw and felt her inner spirit, the gentle and quiet spirit that never complained or blamed God for a drug-dependent husband who wasn't working. She was absolutely beautiful. God honored her heart. Today Jeanette has victory in her life and so does her husband.

*Father God, I so want a quiet and gentle spirit.*
*I'm tired of living in a stressed-out world full of*
*unfinished business. Thanks for Your help. Amen.*

# The Lord Is My Shepherd

**Scripture Reading:** Psalm 23:1-6
**Key Verse:** Psalm 23:4

*Even though I walk through the valley of the shadow
of death, I will fear no evil, for you are with me;
your rod and your staff, they comfort me.*

*I*t was a cool February evening in California. My
88-year-old Jewish auntie's hospital room had its
lights dimmed to gray. It had been a few days since I had
seen her. We had had such a nice visit then. She was alert
as we talked about family and how she missed Uncle
Hy, who had passed away nine months earlier. Now she
lay there so thin and frail. Her breathing was heavy and
irregular.

As I sat by her bedside, holding her cool, clammy
hand, I thought of the other times I had seen her in
similar situations. Auntie had had surgery 25 years
earlier, and because of complications, she almost died.
A few years later she was a passenger in a car that rolled

down a steep hill and hit a power pole. Her face had been smashed, her jaw and nose broken, and other complications set in. Again, she almost died. As life went on, illnesses came and went, but mostly came. The doctors had already told us three times in the past year that Auntie wouldn't make it through the night. But she always did. Was this February night going to be any different? The doctor had been in to check on her and just shook his head. The rabbi arrived to look in for a visit with no response from Auntie. Would this be the night she would give up her fight for life?

On the other side of the curtain that was three-quarters drawn between us and the bed on the other half of the room there was a charming, late-middle-aged Jamaican woman who was almost blind and suffered from diabetes. She spoke eight languages and had a sweet sense of peace and joy about her in spite of her pain. We enjoyed talking with her and found out that she was a Christian believer who grew up learning to read from the Bible. Every night before she closed her eyes to sleep she would recite Psalm 23. On sleepless nights she would repeat it over and over again. As she talked, I felt our spirits meet, and she would tell me how Auntie's day had gone. In only a few hours with her I knew I loved that woman.

Bob and I were both tired as the clock read 11 P.M. that February night. We'd had a busy day in the office and had driven almost two hours through Los Angeles traffic to be with Auntie.

By now Auntie's breathing was very labored. I leaned over to pat her forehead and give her a last hug goodbye. My lips were by her ear when the Spirit of God began to speak from my lips, "The Lord is my Shepherd, I shall not want." Then the angel from "bed B" joined me: "He makes me lie down in green pastures." It was like the sound of a million voices surrounding the room. "Even though I walk through the valley of the shadow of death, I will fear no evil, for you are with me; your rod and your staff, they comfort me." That precious black woman and I dueted to the end of the psalm. "You prepare a table before me in the presence of my enemies. You anoint my head with oil; my cup overflows. Surely goodness and love will follow me all the days of my life, and I will dwell in the house of the Lord forever."

With a last kiss Bob and I walked out of the hospital room forever. Thirty minutes later Auntie died, with the words of the Twenty-third Psalm surrounding her room.

*Father God, I do want to trust in You*
*during all the various times of my life.*
*Help me to realize in good health that You*
*are my shepherd so that in bad times I can*
*trust You to take care of me. You are such a*
*wonderful guardian of all of my life. Amen.*

## A Heritage from the Lord

**Scripture Reading:** Psalm 127:1–128:4

**Key Verse:** Psalm 127:3

*Sons are a heritage from the Lord,*
*children a reward from him.*

In a recent Bible study that I was in, the teacher asked us, "Did you feel loved by your parents when you were a child?" Many remarked:

- "They were too busy for me."
- "I spent too much time with the babysitters."
- "Dad took us on trips, but he played golf all the time we were away."
- "I got in their way. I wasn't important to them."
- "Mom was too involved at the country club to spend time with us."
- "Mom didn't have to work, but she did just so she wouldn't have to be home with us children."

- "A lot of pizzas came to our house on Friday nights when my parents went out for the evening."

I was amazed at how many grown women expressed ways they *didn't* feel loved in their homes growing up. What would your children's answers be if someone asked them the same question?

Today's Scripture reading gives an overview of what it takes to make and develop a close-knit and healthy family. We first look at the foundation of the home in verse 1: "Unless the LORD builds the house, its builders labor in vain. Unless the LORD watches over the city, the watchmen stand guard in vain."

The protective wall surrounding a city was the very first thing to be constructed when a new city was built. The men of the Old Testament knew they needed protection from the enemy, but they were also smart enough to know that walls could be climbed over, knocked down, or broken apart. Ultimately, the people knew that their real security was the Lord guarding the city.

Today we must return to that trust in the Lord, if we are going to be able to withstand the destruction of our "walls"—the family. As I drive the Southern California freeways, I see parents who are burning the candle at both ends to provide for all the material things they think will make their families happy. We rise early and retire late. In Psalm 127:2 we find this is futile. Our trust must be that the Lord has His hand over our families. The business of our hands is only futile effort to satisfy those we love.

In verse 3 we see that, "Children are a reward [gift] from the LORD." In the Hebrew, "gift" means "property," "a possession." Truly, God has loaned us His property or possessions to care for and to enjoy for a certain period of time.

My Bob loves to grow vegetables in his "raised-bed" garden each summer. I am amazed at what it takes to get a good crop. He cultivates the soil, sows seeds, waters, fertilizes, weeds, and prunes. Raising children takes a lot of time, care, nurturing, and cultivating as well. We can't neglect these responsibilities if we are going to produce good fruit. Left to itself, the garden—and our children— will grow into weeds.

Bob always has a big smile on his face when he brings a big basket full of corn, tomatoes, cucumbers, and beans into the kitchen. As the harvest is Bob's reward, so children are parents' reward.

As we move on to Psalm 127:4-5, we see a picture of how to handle our children. They are compared to arrows in the hands of a warrior. Skill in handling an arrow is vital. Wise parents will know their children, understand them, and examine them before they shoot them into the world. When I was in high school, I took an archery class and I soon learned that I wasn't Robin Hood. I found archery much more difficult than basketball, and it was more dangerous if not done properly. Shooting a straight arrow and hitting a target was a lot harder in real life than what I saw at the movies or on

TV. Proper parenting takes a lot of skill. It's not a one-shot experience.

In our last section of this passage, Psalm 128:1-3, we dwell upon the importance of the Lord's presence in the home.

- The Lord is central to a home's happiness (verse 2).
- Through the Lord, wives will be a source of beauty and life to the home (verse 3a).
- Through the Lord, children will flourish like olive trees, which generously provide food, oil, and shelter for others (verse 3b).

Let your home reflect a place where its members come to be rejuvenated after a very busy time away from it. Say "no" when you are tempted to just become a harried taxi driver, delivering the family from one activity to the next. God has a better plan. He wants you to walk in His ways.

*Father God, slow me down so I can spend valuable time with my family. Help me to realize that our children will only be with us for such a short time, and that what I do to and with them will affect their children's lives too. What an awesome responsibility! I can't wait to be with them today. Amen.*

# Choose to Be Thankful

**Scripture Reading:** Ephesians 5:15-20
**Key Verse:** Ephesians 5:20

*…always giving thanks to God the Father for everything, in the name of our Lord Jesus Christ.*

*I* love to travel. In our ministry, I get the great opportunity to travel to various regions in America and Canada. While in the South and Midwest, I love to have the children come up and address me, "Miss Emilie" and to offer a polite gesture of "thank you." It not only tells me a lot regarding the child and that region of our country, but also the teaching that the parent has given to that child.

I would do almost anything for a person who has proper manners and a thankful heart. And if I'm that way as a human being, how much more God must be overjoyed when one of His children responds with a thankful heart. There are two kinds of people in the world: the givers and the takers. It seems like today there are more takers than ever before. We drastically need people with thankful hearts.

In Galatians 5:22 we read a list of Christian characteristics that are universally known as the "fruit of the Spirit." They are: love, joy, peace, patience, kindness, goodness, faithfulness, gentleness, and self-control. Being thankful is not on this list. Evidently to be thankful comes about by choice. We *choose* to be thankful. Have you made that choice today?

We're encouraged to be "always giving thanks to God...for everything" (Ephesians 5:20). That means everything from the littlest to the biggest. I have made thanksgiving a part of my lifestyle. In the morning upon waking, I thank God for another day, for my health, and for purpose for life. In the evening upon retiring, I thank God for watching over me, giving me a meaningful day, and providing safety, food, and shelter. The psalmist expresses it like this, "To proclaim your love in the morning and your faithfulness at night" (Psalm 92:2).

An example of a lady who understands the true meaning of having a thankful heart is reflected in this short excerpt:

The room is clean, even airy; a bright little fire burns in the grate; and in a four-post bed you will see sitting up a woman of sixty-four years of age, with her hands folded and contracted, and her whole body crippled and curled together as the disease cramped it, and rheumatism has fixed it for eight and twenty years. For sixteen of these years, she has not moved from her bed, or looked out of the window, or even lifted her hand to her own face; and also is in constant pain, while she cannot move a limb. But listen! She is so thankful that God has left her that great blessing, the use of one thumb! Her left hand is clinched and stiff, and utterly useless; but she has a two-pronged fork fastened to a stick, with which she can take off her great old-fashioned spectacles, and put them on again, with amazing effort. By the same means, she can feed herself; and she can sip her tea through a tube, helping herself with this one thumb. And there is another thing she can accomplish with her fork; she can turn over the leaves of a large Bible when placed within her reach. A recent visitor addressed her with the remark, that she was all alone. "Yes," she replied in a peculiarly sweet and cheerful voice, "I am alone, and yet not alone."—"How is that?"—"I feel that the Lord is constantly with me."—"How long have you lain here?"—"For sixteen years and four months; and for two years and four months I have not been lifted out of my bed to have it made: yet I have much to praise and bless the Lord for."—"What is the source of your happiness?"—"The thought that my sins are forgiven, and dwelling on the great love of Jesus my Savior. I am content to lie here so long as it shall please Him that I should stay, and to go whenever He shall call me."

Here is a truly divine example of a woman with a thankful heart. Start today if you aren't already—be thankful.

*Father God, bring to my mind all that I need to be thankful for. I sometimes get so hurried and hassled that I don't still my heart and know that You are God. At this moment I say thank You, thank You. Amen.*

# A Treasure in Jars of Clay

**Scripture Reading:** 2 Corinthians 4:7; 6:3-10
**Key Verse:** 2 Corinthians 4:7

*But we have this treasure in jars of clay to show that this all-surpassing power is from God and not from us.*

When our son, Brad, was in high school he really enjoyed taking courses in ceramics. Even though I am his mother, I can say he was very good. In fact, many of his prized vases, jars, and pots still adorn our home. Brad loved working in clay. When I looked at a lump of reddish tan clay, I was always amazed that Brad was able to make a beautiful vessel out of it. When he added color and a glaze, it became a masterpiece.

In today's Scripture we read that we are "jars of clay." We have a great treasure in us, and this all-surpassing power is from God and not from us.

We live in a world that tells us that if we are righteous enough we can become little gods. However, our reading says that we (Christians) are jars of clay with this great treasure (Jesus Christ) in us. I can go to any nursery in our area and purchase an inexpensive clay pot. They're not of much value. On the other hand my dictionary defines "treasure" as wealth or riches, valuable things. Isn't it amazing we hide our treasures in vaults or safe deposit boxes, but God trusts His treasure in a common clay pot? The only value our clay pot has is in the treasure inside.

I am continually amazed how God can use me, just an ordinary person who is willing to be used for Christ's sake. Basic Christianity is simply stated as Jesus Christ, the treasure, in a clay pot, the Christian. If that is true, and I believe it to be true, then I want to share that valuable treasure inside of me with others.

We need to show others that this all-surpassing power is from God and not from us. Philippians 4:13 states, "I can do everything through him who gives me strength." Can you trust God today to believe that you, a clay pot with a great treasure inside, can do all things because Christ Jesus has given you the strength and power to do it? If we, as women, could believe this promise, we would change ourselves, our families, our churches, our cities, our country, and the world. Trust God today for this belief.

*Father God, even though I am an inexpensive clay pot, You make me valuable because You live in me. Thank You for that gift. Amen.*

# Asking the Right Questions

**Scripture Reading:** Romans 8:28-39

**Key Verse:** Romans 8:28

*And we know that in all things God works for the good of those who love him, who have been called according to his purpose.*

In doing radio and TV interviews across America and Canada, I have an opportunity to answer a lot of questions. In my earlier days of ministry, I would just immediately answer the interviewer's questions, assuming I knew exactly what he or she meant. In many cases, I answered the wrong question. Bob would very gently instruct me by saying, "Emilie, you need to ask one more question *before* you answer the question." I started to do that. I know now I'm better able to answer the proper question, and I find my interviews go much more smoothly. There is also definitely clearer communication with my audience.

In our passage for today, Paul asks some very strong

questions that need to be answered from the proper perspective. It is one thing to ask a good question, but getting the right answer is extremely important.

Let's take a look at the questions and the answers that were mentioned in today's reading.

1. "What, then, shall we say in response to this?" (verse 29). *Answer:* In today's passage Paul writes one of the great promises in the New Testament: "And we know that in all things God works for the good of those who love him, who have been called according to his purpose" (verse 28).

- God foreknew us.

- God predestined us to be conformed to the likeness of His son.

- God called us.

- God justified us.

- God glorified us.

What, then, shall we say in response to this? I'm overwhelmed that we have such a marvelous God, one who would do all this for me.

2. "If God is for us, who can be against us?" (verse 31). *Answer:* If I know God, nothing, absolutely nothing, can be taken from me that has any value. We have everything in God through His Son Jesus.

3. "He who did not spare his own Son, but gave him up for us all—how will he not also, along with him, graciously give us all things?" (verse 32). *Answer:* The

blessed answer is that He will graciously give us all things according to His will for our lives. What an assurance to know that what we have has been screened by our heavenly Father.

4. "Who will bring charges against those whom God has chosen?" (verse 33). *Answer:* No one—absolutely no one.

5. "Who is he that condemns?" (verse 34). *Answer:* No one. Jesus Christ is at the right hand of God and is also interceding for us.

6. "Who shall separate us from the love of Christ?" (verse 35). *Answer:* No one. Neither death nor life. Neither angels nor demons. Neither the present nor the future. Neither height nor depth. Nor powers. Nor anything else in all creation. Nothing will be able to separate us from the love of God that is in Christ Jesus our Lord. We can be assured that our questions will be properly answered in Scripture. Try not to rely on the answers of the world, but go to Scripture to get the best answers. And be assured that all things work for our good if we are called according to His purpose.

*Father God, You have answered my number one question: What is my purpose in life? The answer is to serve You with all of my heart. Thank You for giving me the proper answer! Amen.*

# Create in Me a New Heart

**Scripture Reading:** Ezekiel 36:24-27
**Key Verse:** Ezekiel 36:26a

*I will give you a new heart and put a new spirit in you.*

As you begin to meet with God and spend time with Him regularly, you will realize that, with your old heart, you can't do what is necessary to make you a godly person. In fact, none of us can make that transformation happen under our own power—and, fortunately, we don't have to. In Ezekiel 36:26, God says, "I will give you a new heart and put a new spirit in you." God offers us a heart transplant, one that is even more remarkable than a medical transplant of a physical heart.

Thankfully, not every one of us will need a new physical heart, but each of us does need a new spiritual heart. Why? Because we are born with a sinful nature. King David acknowledges that fact in the psalms: "Behold, I was brought forth in iniquity, and in sin my mother conceived me" (51:5). The prophet Jeremiah writes: "The heart is deceitful above all things and beyond cure" (Jeremiah 17:9). Jesus teaches that same lesson: "Out of the heart come evil thoughts, murders, adulteries, fornications, thefts, false witness, slanders" (Matthew 15:19). The apostle Paul wrestles with his sin nature:

"For the good that I wish, I do not do; but I practice the very evil that I do not wish. But if I am doing the very thing I do not wish, I am no longer the one doing it, but sin which dwells in me" (Romans 7:19-20). And the apostle John is very direct in his statement about sin: "If we say that we have no sin, we are deceiving ourselves, and the truth is not in us" (1 John 1:8).

So what are we to do? Not even the most skilled physician can cure a sinful heart or give us a new and pure one. But God can and, according to His promise, will. In *Seeing Yourself Through God's Eyes*, June Hunt talks about this process:

Slowly, after this divine transplant, healing begins and, as promised, your new heart becomes capable of perfect love. Your self-centeredness is now Christ-centeredness. There is healing to replace the hatred; there is a balm for the bitterness. You can face the world with a freedom and a future you have never known before.

"Create in me a clean heart, O God, and renew a steadfast spirit within me" (Psalms 51:10). Once you have a changed heart, you have a changed life. You can love the unlovable, be kind to the unkind, and forgive the unforgivable. All this because you have a new heart—you have God's heart![11]

This kind of heart operation, at the loving hands of your divine Physician, doesn't require major medical insurance. There are no disclaimers or deductibles. God offers this transformation to us free of charge. It costs Him greatly—He gave His only Son for our salvation—but it's a gift to us. All we have to do is accept it—no strings attached.

*Father God, You know that I need a new heart—not one that a doctor transplants but one You change. Give me that newness of spirit that refreshes like the spring water which flows through the valley. Amen.*

# The Two Shall Become One

**Scripture Reading:** Genesis 2:20a-25
**Key Verse:** Genesis 2:24

*For this reason a man will leave his father and mother*
*and be united to his wife, and they will become one flesh.*

One of Aesop's fables tells the story of a wise father who sensed disharmony among his sons and decided to bring them together to discuss this strife. He told each of his four sons to bring a twig to the meeting.

As the young men assembled, the father took each boy's twig and easily snapped it in half. Then he gathered four twigs, tied them together in a bundle, and asked each son to try to break the bundle. Each one tried to no avail. The bundle would not snap.

After each son had tried valiantly to break the bundle, the father asked his boys what they had learned from the demonstration. The oldest son said, "If we are individuals, anyone can break us, but if we stick together, no one can harm us." The father said, "You are right. You must always stand together and be strong."

What is true for the four brothers is equally true for a husband and wife. If we don't stand together and let God make us one in spite of our differences, we will easily be defeated.

As I studied today's Scripture passage, I saw God calling a husband and wife to:

- *departure* ("A man shall leave his father and mother...")
- *permanence* ("And shall cleave to his wife...")
- *oneness* ("And they shall become one flesh")

All three steps must be taken if a marriage is to stand strong.

In God's sight, we become one at the altar when we say our vows to one another before Him. But practically speaking, oneness between a husband and wife is a process that happens over a period of time, over a lifetime together.

Becoming one with another person can be a very difficult process. It isn't easy to change from being independent and self-centered to sharing every aspect of your life and self with another person. The difficulty is often intensified when you're older and more set in your ways when you marry or, as was the case for Bob and me, when the two partners come from very different family, religious, or financial backgrounds. I, for instance, came from an alcoholic family and was raised by a verbally and physically abusive father. Bob came from a warm, loving family where yelling and screaming simply didn't happen. It took us only a few moments to say our vows and enter into oneness in God's eyes, but we have spent more than 50 years blending our lives and building the oneness that we enjoy today.

Becoming one doesn't mean becoming the same, however. Oneness means sharing the same degree of commitment to the Lord and to the marriage, the same goals and dreams, and the same mission in life. Oneness is internal conformity to one another, not an external conformity. It's not the Marines with their short hair-cuts, shiny shoes, straight backs, and characteristic walk. The oneness and internal conformity of a marriage rela-tionship comes with the unselfish act of allowing God to shape us into the marriage partner He would have us be. Oneness results when two individuals reflect the same Christ. Such spiritual oneness produces tremendous strength and unity in a marriage and in the family.

The two marriage partners must leave their fami-lies and let God make them one. Men help the cleaving happen when they show—not just tell—their wives that they are the most important priority after God. Likewise, a wife needs to let her husband know how important he is to her. Your man cannot be competing with your father or any other male for the number-one position in your life. He must know that you respect, honor, and love him if he is to act out his proper role as husband confidently. Your clear communication of your love for him will strengthen the bond of marriage.

Consider what Paul writes to the church at Philippi: "Make my joy complete by being of the same mind, maintaining the same love, united in spirit, intent on one purpose" (Philippians 2:2). This verse has guided me as I worked to unite my family in purpose, thought, and deed. After many years of trial, error, and endless hours of searching, I can say that we are truly united in our purpose and direction. If you were to ask Bob to state our purpose and direction, his answer would match mine: Matthew 6:33—"Seek first his kingdom and his righteousness, and all these things will be given to you." As we have faced decisions through the years, we have asked ourselves, "Are we seeking God's kingdom and His righteousness? Will doing this help us find His kingdom and experience His righteousness? Or are we seeking our own edification or our own satisfaction?" We both hold to this standard whenever we have to decide an issue, and that oneness of purpose helps make our marriage work.

Larry Crabb points out another important dimension to the oneness of a husband and wife when he writes, "The goal of oneness can be almost frightening when we realize that God does not intend [only] that my wife and I find our personal needs met in marriage. He also wants our relationship to validate the claims of Christianity to a watching world as an example of the power of Christ's redeeming love to overcome the divisive effects of sin." [12]

The world does not value permanence and oneness in a marriage, and much of our culture works to undermine those characteristics. But knowing what God intends marriage to be, working to leave, cleave, and become one with our spouse, will help us shine God's light in a very dark world.

*Father God, today's reading has made me aware that there are several areas in my life where my husband and I need better unity. Please give me a proper sensitivity to these areas when I approach him. You know that I want total oneness in purpose of spirit. I thank You now for what You are going to do in this situation. Amen.*

# Your Husband's Friend

**Scripture Reading:** Genesis 2:18-23
**Key Verse:** Genesis 2:18

*The LORD God said, "It is not good for the man to be alone. I will make a helper, suitable for him."*

*G*enesis 2:18-23 is a beautiful picture of how God created not only the first woman and wife, but also the first friend. A wife is indeed to be her husband's friend, and that has truly been my experience. Through the years, the love Bob and I have for each other has grown, and we have become each other's best friend. This passage from Genesis suggests that is exactly what God intends for a married couple. Let's look closely at this section of Scripture.

God gives the woman to the man to be "a helper, suitable for him" (2:18). Do you consider yourself a helper or a hindrance to your husband? To his work? To his time at home? Are you "suitable" or unsuitable when it comes to recognizing and meeting his needs? Where could you be more helpful to him? If you're not sure, why not ask him?

God creates woman from man's rib (2:21-22). Earlier in Genesis, we learn that God created human beings in His image (1:27). The fact that each of us is created in God's image calls us to honor and respect one another. Consider for a moment that your husband was made by God in His image, just as you were. How, then, should you treat him? Acknowledging that your husband has been created in the image of God calls you, I believe, to respect and honor him and to offer him love and friendship.

Adam perceived Eve as part of his own bone and own flesh (2:23). If, like Adam, I rightly understand that Bob is actually part of me, I will want to treat him as well as I treat myself. I will want to take good care of him and provide for his every need. This kind of wife's love provides a good foundation for the kind of friendship a wife can give her man.

Consider the following definition of a friend.

And what is a friend? Many things...a friend is someone you are comfortable with, someone whose company you prefer. A friend is someone you can count on—not only for support, but for honesty.

A friend is one who believes in you...someone with whom you can share your dreams. In fact, a real friend is a person you want to share all of life with...and the sharing doubles the fun.

When you are hurting and you can share your struggle with a friend, it eases the pain. A friend offers you safety and trust...whatever you say will never be used against you.

A friend will laugh with you, but not at you. A friend will pray with you...and for you.

My friend is one who hears my cry of pain, who senses my struggle, who shares my lows as well as my highs.[13]

In such a friendship, nothing is hidden. Such friendship is built on trust, and such friendship takes time to grow and develop. What better context for this kind of friendship to grow than your marriage? How does your marriage measure up against this description? If you and your husband don't yet share this kind of friendship, don't wait for him to reach out. Take the initial step and see how he responds. If you have tried before and not been well received, ask God to guide and bless your efforts and then risk reaching out again.

*Father God, I want You to know that I want to be a friend to my husband. I want to*

fulfill the role for which I was made. Let my
husband know that my desires for him come
from my friendship with him and not from
wanting to take away his freedom. Amen.

# Worthy of Love

**Scripture Reading:** Matthew 22:36-40

**Key Verse:** Matthew 22:37-39

*"Love the Lord your God with all your heart and with all your soul and with all your mind." This is the first and greatest commandment. And the second is like it: "Love your neighbor as yourself."*

Jesus' words in today's key verse are from Deuteronomy 6:4-9. The Jewish nation used these words as part of their Shema, which became Judaism's basic confession of faith. According to rabbinic law, this passage was to be recited every morning and night. This passage stresses the uniqueness of God, precludes the worship of other gods, and demands a total love commitment.

In Matthew 22 Jesus was asked, "Teacher, which is the greatest commandment in the Law?" Jesus gave two commandments which stress three loves: the love of God, the love of your neighbor, and the love of self. We know we ought to love God and to be kind and love our neighbors, but somehow we have a difficult time knowing how to love ourselves. I have met many women who do not understand this concept. As women, we always seem to be giving so much to others in our family that there is no time left for us.

As a young woman and a new bride, then as a new mother, I was always tired. I had no energy left over for me and we most certainly didn't have any money left over from our budget to give me anything. So what did I do for myself? Not very much. After studying this passage of Scripture, I was challenged to study the subject of personal worth. I was careful not to put an overemphasis on self, but to take a balanced and moderate approach that would let me grow as an individual. I knew if God was going to make me a complete and functioning person in the body of Christ, I had to develop a wholesome approach to this area of caring for myself.

As I began to look about me, I discovered women who had a mistrust of themselves and who had begun to withhold love and self-acceptance, women who had no idea that God had a plan for their life, women whose lives reflected fear, guilt, and mistrust of other people. These women did not understand that God had given them certain divine dignity which could make it possible for them to love themselves, and realize they are worthy of love. I also noticed that women would relate to their friends, their husbands, and their children either positively or negatively depending how well they understood this principle.

I can remember one Friday morning in a home Bible

study. We were studying a marriage book, and Amy spoke up and said that she didn't take care of her personal self because her father had told her at a young age that pretty girls with good clothes and nice figures stood a better chance of being molested by older boys and men as they grew up. At that time Amy decided she would not let herself be molested by an older man, so she began to gain weight and wear sloppy clothes. She even remarked that her husband liked her this way because other men didn't try to flirt with her. He felt safe from any competition.

Over the next several months in our weekly study, I began to share with Amy how this fear was put there by Satan and not by God. I took extra time encouraging her to be all that God had for her. We looked at her eating habits and why she chose certain foods. After a while she began to seek professional counseling to understand what she was hiding behind. If you could see Amy today, you would see a fine young woman who has a totally new image and who shares with other women in full confidence. Because of Amy's appropriate self-appraisal, her husband has also joined a support group at church and has lessened his fears from his own insecurities.

What is anger? What is hatred? It is really fear. And what is fear? It is a feeling of being threatened, a deep feeling of insecurity. And what causes that feeling of insecurity? It is a lack of confidence in our ability to cope with threatening situations. And lack of self-confidence is the result of too low a value of yourself. You aren't able to love yourself because of what you think you are!

R.C. Sproul says that "lack of faith" is a "lack of trust" that God is capable of doing what He has promised He will do.

It takes a lot of faith to love. People who cannot love themselves do not dare to love. They are afraid they'll be spurned or rejected. Why do they have that fear? Because they do not trust themselves or rate themselves high enough to believe they'll be loved. And why do they fear rejection? Because rejection will only put salt in the wounds, proving again that they aren't worthy.

In Genesis 1:26-27 it says, "Then God said, 'Let us make man in our image, in our likeness...' So God created man in his own image, in the image of God he created him; male and female he created them." In verse 31 the Scripture says, "God saw all that he had made, and it was very good." We were spiritually designed to enjoy the honor that befits a prince of heaven. There is a basic need to recognize the dignity of the human being to be a child of God.

George Gallup, Jr., of the Gallup organization, conducted a poll on the self-esteem of the American public. The poll conclusively demonstrated that people with a positive self-image demonstrate the following qualities:

1. They have a high moral and ethical sensitivity.

2. They have a strong sense of family.

3. They are far more successful in interpersonal relationships.

4. Their perspective of success is viewed in terms of interpersonal relationships, not in crass materialistic terms.

5. They're far more productive on the job.

6. They are far lower in incidents of chemical addictions. (Current research shows that 80 percent of all suicides are related to alcohol and drug addiction.)

7. They are more likely to get involved in social and political activities in their community.

8. They are far more generous to charitable institutions and give far more generously to relief causes.[14]

As contributing members of our family, church, community, and society, each of us wants these positive qualities.

It seems the majority of our churches struggle in implementing the three loves of Deuteronomy and Matthew. But people who view God as a personal, loving, and forgiving Being, and relate to Him in such a personal way, do develop a strong, healthy sense of self-worth. Make sure you are in a church that teaches these aspects of the gospel.

Paul teaches in Philippians 4:13 that, "I can do

everything through him who gives me strength." Using this principle, we can realize that Christ gives us the inner strength to care for ourselves. We must choose to love ourselves. There are many who say that self-love is evil and wrong, but I don't believe that's true. I want to encourage you to take time for yourself each day. Time for yourself gives you time to renew your mind, body, and spirit. Not only will you be rewarded, but so will those who come in contact with you daily.

*Father God, I don't want to become self-centered, but I do want to understand the value You have given me because You gave Your Son. Please reveal to me those areas of my life that I find difficult to love. Help me to base my sense of self-worth on You. Amen.*

# Continually Seek God's Wisdom

**Scripture Reading:** Proverbs 1:1-7

**Key Verse:** Proverbs 1:7

*The fear of the Lord is the beginning of knowledge,*
*but fools despise wisdom and discipline.*

If you go to God looking for knowledge and wisdom, you'll find it—and the wisdom that comes from God is the kind that will protect you. God is the giver of all good things. It just makes sense to listen as He speaks!

A lot of people have the idea that following God is a big burden. But that's not the way it works in real life. Actually, when you open your heart to receive wisdom from God, you'll find that it's a pleasing thing. It actually feels good to be guided by God and follow His paths.

…The more you experience doing what is right, the clearer your decisions of right and wrong will become. It starts out with the glimmer of the faint light of daybreak—you get a little sense of what is right and you act on it. As you continue to make right decisions (using the words of Scripture and dependable counselors to help you), everything becomes a lot clearer and brighter and less confusing. What once seemed murky and hard to distinguish takes on the intensity of the noonday sun. So don't worry if you sometimes seem to be walking along dimly lit paths. Keep on doing what you know to be right, and everything will get a lot clearer. There's no reason to stumble when wisdom provides the light.

…Sometimes it seems as if the world rewards the wrong people! Public immorality, official corruption, random violence, and just plain bad manners almost seem the standard of success, and the sleaziest, most indecent people seem to be making money, gaining fame, and being elected to office.

But don't be fooled. In the end, your attempt to… live out the life that God has designed will be rewarded. By your very life, you'll add to the joy in your family, neighborhood, city, state, and nation—not to mention the joy that fills the heavens.[15]

Solomon's wise sayings offer us advice on how to conduct ourselves in various situations in everyday life. His fundamental instruction is to fear and trust the Lord. Solomon challenges us to continually seek God's wisdom in the decisions we must make each day.

This type of knowledge goes beyond academic accomplishments to moral responsibility. It focuses in on decision-making and shows itself best in the disciplining of our character. We raise our children to be lawyers, doctors, teachers, sales people, musicians, but do we ever purposefully raise our children to be good? We need a country where parents want to raise children to be good. Our country and world are desperately in need of good people.

We must begin to think clearly and scripturally if we are to survive the present cultural war in America. In regard to right and wrong, we must arrive at consistent answers that go along with our theological understanding of Scripture. We can't be swayed by what the secular world says. We must go to Scripture to see what God instructs us to do (see Romans 12:12). We must continually seek God's wisdom.

*Father God, I want to be a woman who seeks after Your knowledge. Show me Your ways that I might acknowledge You as God. Help me to see that You are all that I will ever need. Amen.*

# Dwelling in the Sanctuary

**Scripture Reading:** Psalm 15:1-5
**Key Verse:** Psalm 15:1-5

*LORD, who may dwell in your sanctuary? Who may live on your holy hill? He whose walk is blameless and who does what is righteous, who speaks the truth from his heart and has no slander on his tongue, who does his neighbor no wrong and casts no slur on his fellowman, who despises a vile man but honors those who fear the LORD, who keeps his oath even when it hurts, who lends his money without usury and does not accept a bribe against the innocent. He who does these things will never be shaken.*

*I*n today's passage David describes the character of the person who qualifies to be a guest of God's sanctuary. The two parallel questions of verse 1 are answered in the following four verses by an eleven-fold description of the righteous person who is upright in deed, word and attitude, and finances. These qualities, which aren't natural, are imparted by God and by His Holy Spirit.

Let's see what we can learn from this great psalm about the person who may dwell in the Lord's sanctuary:

1. He walks blameless.
2. He does what is righteous.
3. He speaks the truth from his heart.
4. He has no slander on his tongue.
5. He does his neighbor no harm.
6. He casts no slur on his fellowman.
7. He despises a vile (evil) man.
8. He honors those who fear the Lord.
9. He keeps his oath even when it hurts.
10. He lends his money without usury.
11. He does not accept a bribe against the innocent.

These are honorable characteristics! We certainly can appreciate the virtue of this type of person. However, many times we look upon the life of a righteous person and say to ourselves, "It must be easy for her to be a Christian. She evidently doesn't have the struggles with sin like I do!" Yet anyone who is trying to live a righteous life knows that we must choose each day to serve the Lord. It isn't any easier for any of us. We must decide moment by moment to do what is right.

David closes this psalm by stating, "He who does these things will never be shaken." What a great promise. Now let's live it with great faith.

*Father God, the Scripture tells me to dwell on those things which are honorable and pure in deed. I willfully decide today to believe and live the Scriptures as the saints of old, beginning with precept unto precept and line upon line. I want to be Your woman. Amen.*

# Believe What God Believes About You

**Scripture Reading:** 1 Corinthians 13:4-13
**Key Verse:** 1 Corinthians 13:4-13

*Love is patient, love is kind. It does not envy, it does not boast, it is not proud. It is not rude, it is not self-seeking, it is not easily angered, it keeps no record of wrongs. Love does not delight in evil but rejoices with the truth. It always protects, always trusts, always hopes, always perseveres.*

*Love never fails. But where there are prophecies, they will cease; where there are tongues, they will be stilled; where there is knowledge, it will pass away. For we know in part and we prophesy in part, but when perfection comes, the imperfect disappears. When I was a child, I talked like a child, I thought like a child, I reasoned like a child. When I became a man, I put childish ways behind me. Now we see but a poor reflection as in a mirror; then we shall see face to face. Now I know in part; then I shall know fully, even as I am fully known.*

*And now these three remain: faith, hope and love. But the greatest of these is love.*

*I*t's important to believe that we have value and that we are worthy to give of ourselves. This begins by knowing and accepting what our heavenly Father believes about us. Christian psychologist Dr. Dick Dickerson has written a paraphrase of 1 Corinthians 13 which beautifully summarizes how God looks at us. Read this aloud to yourself each morning and evening for the next 30 days, then evaluate how your feelings about yourself have changed:

- Because God loves me, He is slow to lose patience with me. Because God loves me, He takes the circumstances of my life and uses them in a constructive way for my growth. Because God loves me, He does not treat me as an object to be possessed and manipulated.

- Because God loves me, He has no need to impress me with how great and powerful He is because He is God. Nor does He belittle me as His child in order to show me how important He is.

- Because God loves me, He is for me. He wants me to mature and develop in His love.

- Because God loves me, He does not send down His wrath on every little mistake I make, of which there are many.

- Because God loves me, He does not keep score of all my sins and then beat me over the head with them whenever He gets a chance.

- Because God loves me, He is deeply grieved when I do not walk in the ways that please Him because He sees this as evidence that I don't trust Him and love Him as I should.

- Because God loves me, He rejoices when I experience His power and strength and stand up under the pressure of life for His name's sake.

- Because God loves me, He keeps working patiently with me even when I feel like giving up and can't see why He doesn't give up with me too.

- Because God loves me, He keeps on trusting me when at times I don't even trust myself.

- Because God loves me, He never says there is no hope for me, rather, He patiently works with me, loves me, and disciplines me in such a way that it is hard for me to understand the depth of His concern for me.

- Because God loves me, He never forsakes me even though many of my friends might.[16]

"Please be patient with me. God isn't finished with me yet." That is certainly true! As we look at a particular area in our lives, we can be tempted to break into tears of discouragement because we feel so defeated. But God is still working in our lives, and He will never give up on us.

There is a void in each of our lives that cannot be filled by the world. We may leave God or put Him on hold, but He is always there. He patiently waits for us to run our race, becoming fatigued in the process, and then to turn back to Him.

As you become secure in God's love, you will discover that you need not surrender your caring for yourself to the opinions and judgments of others. God is for you!

*Father God, negative inner voices would love*
*to convince me that I am a nobody, but the*
*Holy Spirit continually challenges me to believe*
*that I am of value to God and will be with*
*Jesus in Paradise. Can I believe God when He*
*tells me that I was so important to Him that*
*He gave His only Son, Jesus Christ, to die on*
*the cross for my sins? Yes, I can! I am special*
*to God. Let me believe it and live it. Amen.*

who cares. At times I sound like a squeaky wheel around my children and family. But You know that I want the very best for them. I want them to know of Your love for them, how to live a disciplined life, to be responsible for their actions, and how to have a healthful selection of foods. Even though I may not live to see them grown, I want You to know that my desire is to make them the children You would have them be. Thank You for putting that desire in my heart. Amen.

# One Day at a Time

**Scripture Reading:** Zechariah 4:1-7
**Key Verse:** Zechariah 4:6b

*"Not by might nor by power, but by my
Spirit," says the LORD Almighty.*

*D*ear Mrs. Barnes:

I've just finished reading your book *Survival for Busy Women*. I feel that it helped me a good bit. It's very easy for me to get down because of my daily schedule. I know you're a very busy woman, but if you have a few minutes to look at my average daily schedule and offer any helpful ideas about how to organize my day better so I would have more time to spend with my husband and six-year-old son, I would greatly appreciate it.

I never do any "housecleaning" during the week, and I hardly vacuum the floors on the weekend. Most of the time I just can't stand doing major housecleaning on my only day off (besides Sunday, of course, but I'm not cleaning house on Sunday—that day is filled with church and family).

With a schedule like this, when do I have time to spend with my husband or my child?

This woman leads an active life! I imagine she often feels like a juggler in a circus. Sound familiar to you? Many of us are overwhelmed by the pressures and responsibilities we face, yet we still keep taking on more and more. We have not learned to say "No" to good things and save our "Yeses" for the best.

Are there some good things we are doing which we should say no to? We are not superwomen. The secular world has led us down the path of lies which says, "We can do it all. We can have it all." Very few of us are that capable. We must learn to major on the major issues of life and not get sidetracked on the minors that drain us of all the creativity, energy, and productivity God has given us.

A good way to major on the major issues is to learn to live one day at a time. Go to the Lord each day and seek His guidance and wisdom for today—not tomorrow, not next week, not next year, but today. There is great value in doing a "to-do" list each day as well. On a pad of paper list only those things that need to be done today, not tomorrow or next week, but just today. After a few days of making lists, you will find yourself having to rank your activities by priority, certain things being more important than others. Concentrate on the most important activity first and let the least important items settle to the end of the day. (Some of these will even drop off the page, because of their low priority.) You will be amazed at how much you will accomplish when you do this one project—a to-do list.

At night as you crawl into bed, look at your list, smile, and thank God for helping you stay on schedule. Utter a prayer of thanksgiving that expresses your appreciation for God giving you the power to say no to "minor" requests.

*Father God, I pray for my schedules. I ask*
*for wise discernment in order to gain control*
*of my life. Give me the courage to say "no"*
*to the time wasters and say "yes" to the*
*things that have eternal value. Amen.*

# Great Family Blessings

**Scripture Reading:** Ecclesiastes 4:8-12
**Key Verse:** Ecclesiastes 4:12 (NASB)

*A cord of three strands is not quickly torn apart.*

"I wish I had some good friends to help me in life!" cried lazy Dennis. "Good friends? Why, you have ten!" replied his master. "I'm sure I don't have half that many, and those I have are too poor to help me." "Count your fingers, my boy," said his master. Dennis looked down at his strong hands. "Count thumbs and all," added the master. "I have; there are ten," replied the lad. "Then never say you don't have ten good friends to help you on in life. Try what those true friends can do before you grumble and fret because you do not get help from others."—Source unknown

Many times we look to others to help us out and complain when we don't receive the help we think we deserve. But help starts within ourselves, then moves outward. We need to take an inventory of all the skills and tools that God has so graciously given us at birth. We tend to take for granted those attributes of success which were given to us at the very beginning of our life. Our fingers and thumbs are such valuable tools for work. They truly are our dearest friends. In addition, King Solomon in all his wisdom told us that friends are great blessings to our family. He emphasized in Ecclesiastes chapter 4 (NASB):

- Two are better than one because they have a good return for their labor (verse 9).

- Woe to the one who falls when there is not another to lift him up (verse 10).

- If two lie down together they keep warm (verse 11).

- Two can resist one who tries to overpower them (verse 12a).

- A cord of three strands is not quickly torn apart (verse 12b).

Are you working on relationships that build these kinds of blessings? Begin at home with your family members. Throughout Scripture we are told to be united with one another. Unity should be our goal as husband/wife, parent/child, child/sibling.

Begin to develop those traits that have eternal worth, not the temporal traits that live for such a short time.

In Ecclesiastes 4:8 Solomon asks one of the most

basic questions of life: "For whom am I laboring and depriving myself of pleasure?" Is it all for vanity? Does it have redeeming value to you and your family? If not, do something about it.

*Father God, in my heart and soul I want my family to be a blessing to me, and likewise I want to be a blessing to them. At times it seems to be in vain. Bring to mind those traits that are so important for friendships. I do want to be counted as a friend to those around me. Let me be a discerning person when it comes to doing my best for the people You have placed in my life. Let me major on major issues and minor on minor issues of life. Amen.*

# The Minimum Daily Adult Requirement

**Scripture Reading:** Ephesians 2:4-9
**Key Verse:** Ephesians 2:8-9

*For it is by grace you have been saved, through faith—and this not from yourselves, it is the gift of God—not by works, so that no one can boast.*

A couple of years ago I had a young college student ask me, "How much beer can I drink as a Christian?" Others have asked:

- How long should I read my Bible each day?

- How long should I pray each day?

- How much money do I have to give to the church?

- Do I have to sing in the choir to be a good Christian?

- How many times a week must I be in church?

- Do I have to _____, _____, _____?

On and on we go. We all want to know what the "minimum daily adult requirement" is for being a Christian. What do we *really* have to do, day-by-day, to get by?

Sue Gregg and I have written a lot of cookbooks dealing with God-given principles for a balanced lifestyle regarding food. The American consumer is very sophisticated when it comes to reading labels. Some even have small calculators with them as they stroll the aisle with shopping carts under tow. They can tell you unit costs, what kind of sugar is being used, what the derivative of the fat content is, how many calories, how much sodium, what is the nutritional information per serving, and yes, even the percentages of the minimum daily adult requirement.

If we want to know about the daily requirements in regard to our food, should we not also be concerned about this in our Christian walk? Of course! It only makes sense that we would definitely want to know how long Christians pray, how long they read their Bible, how much money they should put in the offering plate, how many church activities they participate in each week, etc.

Paul addresses these very basic questions in Ephesians. He very clearly states, "For it is by grace you have been saved, through faith—and this not from yourselves, it is the gift of God—not by works, so that no one can boast" (verses 8-9). Christ has freed us from this bondage of minimum daily adult requirements! It is not of works, but of grace.

You might ask, "Do I do nothing as a Christian? Aren't there some requirements?" The Scriptures challenge us to be like Christ. If I am to grow as unto the Lord, I need to study to see what He did and how He did it. For example, I find Him studying the Law. I see Him meeting with other believers. I see Him praying regularly. I see Him serving others around Him in need. I see Him giving to those in need.

Christ did not do them because He was *told* to do them. He did them because He *wanted* to do them. Seek from the Holy Spirit what your minimum daily adult requirement is. It is different for every one of us.

*Father God, help me not to worry about how long or how often. Put a strong desire in my soul to spend time with You today in prayer and study. Let time stand still and let me forget all about my watch and schedule. Amen.*

# If I Had It All to Do Over

**Scripture Reading:** Luke 22:7-20

**Key Verse:** Luke 22:19b (NASB)

*This is My body which is given for you;*
*do this in remembrance of Me.*

Someone asked me the other day if I had my life to live over, would I change anything? My answer was no, but I thought about it and changed my mind. If I had my life to do over again I would have waxed less and listened more.

Instead of wishing away nine months of pregnancy and complaining about the shadows over my feet, I'd have cherished every minute of it and realized that the wonderment growing inside me was to be my only chance in life to assist God in a miracle.

I would never have insisted that the car windows be rolled up on a summer day because my hair had just been teased and sprayed.

I would have invited friends over to dinner even if

the carpet was stained and the sofa faded. I would have eaten popcorn in the "good" living room and worried less about the dirt when you lit the fireplace. I would have taken time to listen to my grandfather ramble about his youth.

I would have burned the pink candle sculptured like a rose before it melted while being stored. I would have sat cross-legged on the lawn with my children and never worried about grass stains.[17] Here is a woman looking back on life and remembering all the little phases and events we often overlook the first time around.

Each of us, regardless of what our ages are, look back with regret that we didn't take more time to _____. My Bob gets melancholy when we see our old photo slides of the children when they were young. He remembers when he could have if he would have. But we can't go back and recapture lost opportunities. We need to take advantage of each day and live it to the fullest.

When we take communion at our church, the elements are placed on a table with these words carved on the side facing the congregation: "This Do in Remembrance of Me." The Scriptures state very clearly that we are to look back to the cross and remember what Christ did for us. At the communion table we are to *break bread* ("This is My body which is given for you; do this in remembrance of Me.") and *drink from the cup* ("This cup which is poured out for you is the new covenant in My blood.").

We are to remember what Christ Jesus did for us in history. Elisabeth Elliot states, "Ultimate hatred and ultimate love met on those two crosspieces of wood. Suffering and love were brought into harmony."

As we look back over our life, let's make sure that we have accepted Jesus as He suffered for us and our sins on the cross and paid the price of His death because of His ultimate love for us. This unselfish act has been the greatest event in human history. As we look back, may we clearly remember Jesus, the bread, and the cup of wine.

*Father God, I remember back to when I was 16 years old; it seemed like just yesterday that I accepted Jesus as my personal Savior. Through that very act You assured me that Jesus was my Messiah of the Old Testament. In one instant I had become a completed Jewish girl. As I remember back I have never regretted the decision I made one night on my knees beside my bed. You have been my strength and support over these years. Without You I fear what might have become of my life. You have been the difference between who I am and what I could have been. Reveal Your Son, Jesus Christ, to other women who are searching for meaning in their lives. Amen.*

*Using Our Talents*

**Scripture Reading:** Matthew 25:14-30
**Key Verse:** Matthew 25:21

*Well done, good and faithful servant!*

This passage contains two important points:

- God's call for faithfulness in the use of our talents to Him.

- A warning for those who do not use their talents.

I am continually amazed as I talk to women across America that so many don't realize God can use ordinary people to spread the gospel to those around them.

As a young child growing up behind my mother's dress store, I had no idea that God could use me for much. It wasn't until many years later that God challenged me to take small steps to venture out into this world called "risks" and to be faithful to this calling.

We often think that our talents are going to come out full-grown. However, it is only as we cultivate them that they become mature. As a young seventh-grade girl,

I took up playing a beautiful string instrument—the cello. Only after several years of hard practice was I able to play second chair in the Long Beach All City Honors Orchestra.

As with any talent, we must be willing to be used. Yes, there is a risk, but it's worth the insecurity to find out how far God can take us if we are willing. In today's parable we see that the first two servants were willing to take that risk. Their stewardship gave them a blessing of 100-percent return for their efforts, plus their master said, "Well done, good and faithful servant! You have been faithful with a few things; I will put you in charge of many things. Come and share your master's happiness!"

If you want to be successful in God's eyes, you must first be faithful with a few things; then God will cheerfully put you in charge of many things. Is there a talent that people keep telling you that you are good at, but you just shrug it off as not being good enough? No one could be blessed by my talent, you think. This passage tells you to take the risk. Don't limit God—He is not to be put into a box. How many of you have a poem to be written, a song to be sung, a book to be authored? Listen to God today as He calls you to a life of adventure. Life is not boring when you have a purpose.

*A warning to those who don't use their talents.* Even though today's passage talks about faithfulness to use our talents for God, we can't leave this Scripture without looking briefly at God's warning in verses 24-30. This third servant was afraid. He wasn't willing to take a risk with his one talent. He went and buried it in the ground. How many of us are fearful and bury our talents? The warning of these few verses is that God holds us responsible for our lives and what we do with them.

We want to stand before God one day and hear Him say, "Well done, good and faithful servant!"

*Father God, at times I don't feel I have any talents, but I know You have given each of Your children special gifts. Today I'm asking for direction in using my talents for Your glory. Thank You for listening to my prayer. Amen.*

*Home Rules*

**Scripture Reading:** Deuteronomy 6:1-9

**Key Verse:** Deuteronomy 6:7a (NASB)

*You shall teach them diligently to your sons.*

*H*ome is the one place in this entire world where hearts are sure of each other. It is the place of confidence. It is the place where we tear off that mask of guarded and suspicious coldness which the world forces us to wear in self-defense, and where we pour out the unreserved communications of full and confiding hearts. It is the spot where expressions of tenderness gush out without any sensation of awkwardness and without any dread of ridicule.[18]

In our Scripture passage today God outlines the responsibility that we have as parents to teach our children at home and in other venues that are appropriate. So important were the commands of the Lord that Moses directed us to do everything possible to remember these commands and to incorporate them into everyday life.

The spiritual education of the children was the responsibility of the parents. The teaching would take place daily through the example of the parents as well as through the repetition of the law. The importance of this command is seen by the extent to which parents were to go in order to teach their children. This was more than simply teaching the facts of the law; it was to be the demonstration of a lifestyle woven into the tapestry (see verses 8-9) of everyday life. Creativity is essential in teaching the precepts of God while we are involved in mundane chores of the household.

### Character and Conduct

Conduct is what we do; character is what we are. Conduct is the outward life; character is the life unseen, hidden within, yet evidenced by that which is seen. Conduct is external, seen from without; character is internal—operating within.... Character is the state of the heart, conduct is its outward expression. Character is the root of the tree, conduct, the fruit it bears.

—E.M. Bounds

Today that becomes our biggest task—to teach Christian values and responsibilities in a creative fashion. How can we compete with TV sound bites, Disney mind-set, computers, and laser printers? We live in an age of fast-paced technology that throws fast, colorful, and short concentration bites of information to all of us, including our children.

It takes creative parenting to teach our young ones biblical principles. Often our children pick up on our walk better than on our talk. They have great discernment in observing how Mom and Dad (and other adults) live out these principles.

In verse 7 we find that teaching and learning doesn't always take place in a formal, rigid classroom setting. We are to talk of these principles when we sit in our house, when we walk by the way, when we lie down, and when we rise.

Twenty-four hours a day we can integrate biblical truths in everyday settings. Ann Landers printed a set of Home Rules from a lady in California:

- If you sleep on it—make it up.
- If you wear it—hang it up.
- If you drop it—pick it up.
- If you eat out of it—put it in the sink.
- If you spill it—wipe it up.
- If you empty it—fill it up.
- If it rings—answer it.
- If it howls—feed it.
- If it cries—love it.[19]

If your children understood these nine simple rules when they started kindergarten, the teacher would sing praises to your name, for these form the basic foundation for citizenship. It is amazing how many adults can't demonstrate these simple, basic manifestations of responsibility.

*Father God, being a godly parent is not easy.
Sometimes I just want to go back to the simple
life without having to face the awesomeness
of raising children. I get so tired and weary of
being the one to transmit virtue values to the
next generation. Restore in my soul the desire to
keep on keeping on. There are some days when
I think it's impossible to continue with what I
feel is an endless task of teaching my children.
Please reassure my faith in what I've set out to
do—to be obedient to Your commands. Amen.*

*God's Gift*

**Scripture Reading:** John 10:10-18
**Key Verse:** John 10:10

*The thief comes only to steal and kill and destroy; I have come that they may have life, and have it to the full.*

One evening we attended a service at an Evangelical Free Church in Fullerton, California. Pastor Chuck Swindoll introduced the speaker for the evening, a man by the name of Ravi Zacharias. His opening statement was "The most dangerous place for a young child today is in his mother's womb." Tears filled my eyes and flooded down my cheeks. I wanted to sob. *Oh, God,* I thought, *what has happened in the world today?* Children are being thrown away as trash, right in our own cities. God says, "Behold, children are a gift of the LORD" (Psalm 127:3 NASB). We aren't even waiting to unwrap the gift, or allowing the fruit of the womb to be God's reward.

When I held our new little grandson, Bradley Joe II, I saw the miracle of God—a child planted and formed by the Almighty. As I watch our children raise their children, God has impressed upon me the desire to teach women to love and care for children. What a blessing of trust that God would count us women worthy to care for one of His dear children!

Our niece, Becky, and her husband, George, adopted a son. They could never have a child from her womb due to cancer in her body at a very early age. God allowed a child to be born to another woman so Becky and George could be the parents they so desired. This child is sent from God, a gift of God. *Thank You, Lord, that this child was not a throwaway, but a child who will contribute much to our society, adopted into a family who wanted a child.*

That's exactly what God has for us. He wants to adopt us into His family. We are not God's throwaways. We are His reward. He said, "I have come to give you life" (John 10:10). God sent His Son Jesus as a sacrificed gift to us. He laid down His life for us. Jesus went to the cross so we will never have to suffer the punishment. He took the sins of the world upon Himself and died for you and me.

*Thank You, Jesus, for Your love to me that while I was yet a sinner, You died for me. Thank You for the little children. Please protect them in their mother's womb, and may these children be an opened gift to parents. May we, as a country, rise up and defend our children in and out of the womb. Amen.*

# Be a Living Presence

**Scripture Reading:** Psalm 127:1-5
**Key Verse:** Psalm 127:3 (NASB)

*Behold, children are a gift of the Lord;*
*the fruit of womb is a reward.*

The young mother asked her guide about the path of life. "Is the way long?" she inquired. And her guide replied: "Yes. And the way is hard. And you will be old before you reach the end of it. But the end will be better than the beginning."

But the young mother was happy, and she would not believe that anything could be better than these years. So she played with her children, and gathered flowers for them along the way, and basked with them in the clear streams; and the sun shone on them and life was good, and the young mother said, "Nothing will ever be lovelier than this."

Then night came, and storm, and the path was dark, and the children shook with fear and cold, and the mother drew them close and covered them with her mantle, and the children said, "Oh, Mother, we are not afraid, for you are near, and no harm can come." And the mother observed, "This is better than the brightness of day, for I have taught my children courage."

And the morning came, and there was a hill ahead, and the children climbed and grew weary, and the mother was weary too, but she said to the children, "A little patience and we are there." So the children climbed, and when they reached the top they said, "We could not have done it without you, Mother." And the mother, when she lay down that night, looked at the stars and said, "This is a better day than the last, for my children have learned fortitude in the face of hardness. Yesterday I gave them courage, and today I have given them strength."

And the next day came strange clouds which darkened the earth—clouds of war and hate and evil, and the children groped and stumbled, and the mother said, "Look up. Lift your eyes to the Light." And the children looked and saw above the clouds an Everlasting Glory, and it guided them and brought them beyond the darkness. And that night the mother said, "This is the best day of all, for I have shown my children God."

And the days went on, and the weeks and the months and the years, and the mother grew old, and she was little and bent. But her children were tall and strong, and walked with courage. And when the way was hard, they helped their mother, and when the way was rough, they lifted her, for she was as light as a feather; and at last they came to a hill, and beyond the hill they could see a shining road and golden gates flung wide.

And the mother said: "I have reached the end of my journey. And now I know that the end is better than the beginning, for my children can walk alone, and their children after them."

And the children said, "You will always walk with us, Mother, even when you have gone through the gates."

And they stood and watched her as she went on alone, and the gates closed after her. And they said: "We cannot see her, but she is with us still. A mother like ours is more than a memory. She is a living presence." [20]

In our society today the most dangerous place for a child to be is in her mother's womb. Who would ever have thought that to be true? Too many women and parents have never known or have forgotten the promise of the Lord that children are a gift: They are the fruit of the womb.

Does this promise just happen, or are there things that we do to earn this promise? No, it doesn't just happen. For a mother to become a "living presence" she must spend time, time, and more time with her children. "Is the way long?" Yes, it is. In fact at times it seems forever.

Young mothers write letters or talk to me completely frustrated with life because the children take so much time from their day. I tell them they won't always be in that phase of their lives. Enjoy the children while they're young, because as they get older both parents and children will have new sets of difficulties.

Each phase of life has challenges that are new to us. I can vividly remember when Bob and I had five children under the age of five and I was only 21 years old. I thought I would never make it. But was it worth it? Yes, it was. I can truly say that children are a gift from God and that they are a fruit from the mother's womb.

I have found that you develop a living presence with your children if you

- raise them at an early age to know Christ personally

- show interest in their friends and activities

- show them that you really love your spouse (if you are married)

- exercise fairness with them in conversation and discipline

- let them grow up without overprotection; let them make mistakes, make decisions, and get bumps and scrapes

- use encouraging words to lift them up

- let them have and express different opinions from your own

- be good role models so they will know their gender roles (boys are to become men and girls are to become women)

- be willing to clearly confess and admit your wrongdoings and ask for forgiveness
- establish firm and clear boundaries

Proverbs 31:10-31 can help you become a capable woman. This passage is an acrostic poem exalting the honor and dignity of womanhood. In verses 30 and 31 we read, "A woman who fears the Lord...shall be praised. Give her the product of her hands, and let her works praise her in the gates."

Is the way long? Yes, and the way is hard. And you will be old before you reach the end of it. But the end will be better than the beginning.

Get on board, for the trip will be a blessing for you and for all those fortunate enough to be in your family!

*Father God, thank You again for the assurance that Your plan works. As I talk to friends, see the news on the TV, and read the newspaper, I get so discouraged about having children. I truly want my children to be a gift from You and the fruit of the womb for me. In turn I also want to be a blessing in their lives. Give me the strength today to set my foot on the path of life. Amen.*

# Godly Examples

**Scripture Reading:** Psalm 78:1-7
**Key Verse:** Psalm 78:4

*We will not hide them [commandments] from
their children; we will tell the next generation
the praiseworthy deeds of the LORD, his
power, and the wonders he has done.*

*A* young father was having a talk with his young
son as they were preparing to get ready for bed.
The father was telling the lad what Christians should
be like and how they should act. When Dad had finished describing the attributes of a Christian, the young
boy asked a stunning question: "Daddy, have I ever seen
a Christian?" The father was aghast. *What kind of an
example am I?* he thought.

How would you feel if your child asked you the same
question? In our reading today we are given some help to
make sure this doesn't happen. This passage establishes
some patterns for parenting, patterns we can use to help
our children know the things of God and to realize that
we are God's children. The writer of Psalm 78 states we

can do this by telling the next generation the praises of the Lord (verse 4) and teaching our children the statutes and laws of God (verse 5). Then our children will see by our words and examples that we are Christians.

In Deuteronomy 6:6-7 Moses said, "These commandments that I give you today are to be upon your hearts. Impress them on your children. Talk about them when you sit at home and when you walk along the road, when you lie down and when you get up."

As parents we are to be reflectors of God to our children. As they look into our faces, our lives, they are to see a man or woman of godly desires and actions. In America today, we earnestly need more parents who will stand up and do the right thing. Christian growth is a daily process of taking off the old self of attitudes, beliefs, and behaviors which reflect the dark side of our nature (sin) and changing to those characteristics that reflect the presence of Christ in our lives. The only way we can grow and succeed in this continuous process is by being renewed in the spirit of our mind (Ephesians 4:22-24). It is a moment-to-moment decision.

By word and by personal example we must train and nurture our children. In this way they can know what a Christian is, because they have known you—the reflector of God's grace.

*Father God, I thank You for the godly men and*

*women You have put in my life. They have been a real inspiration to my Christian growth. Help me to continually seek out those godly people who will live the Christian walk in front of me. Amen.*

*Be a Friend*

**Scripture Reading:** Proverbs 18:20-24
**Key Verse:** Proverbs 18:24b (NASB)

*There is a friend who sticks closer than a brother.*

*A* mouse one day happened to run across the paws of a sleeping lion and wakened him. The lion, angry at being disturbed, grabbed the mouse and was about to swallow him, when the mouse cried out, "Please, kind sir, I didn't mean it; if you will let me go, I shall always be grateful, and perhaps I can help you someday."

The idea that such a little thing as a mouse could help him so amused the lion that he let the mouse go. A week later the mouse heard a lion roaring loudly. He went closer to see what the trouble was and found his lion caught in a hunter's net. Remembering his promise, the mouse began to gnaw the ropes of the net and kept it up until the lion could get free. The lion then acknowledged that little friends might prove to be great friends.
—Aesop

Friends and friendships are unique social happenings. Often I wonder why some people are attracted to others. Is it because of common interest, past experiences, physical attraction, having children who are friends of a potential friend, or going to the same church? What is it that bonds people together? As I consider the many friends I have, I sense it's a little of all of the above. They come from various backgrounds, religions, economic levels, and educational attainment. There does, however, seem to be one common strand that runs through most of these friendships: We have a kindred spirit in the Lord.

The writer of today's proverb gives a warning in the first part of verse 24: "A man of many friends comes to ruin." When I first read that I was confused. I thought to myself, "I thought we were to have a lot of friends, so why this warning?" But as I thought about this, a thought came to me. He was stressing that too many friends chosen indiscriminately will bring trouble, but a genuine friend sticks with you through thick and thin. When we use this criterion for a friend, we begin to thin the ranks of who are truly our friends.

I know without a doubt that several of my friends would be with me no matter what the circumstances, what day of the week, and what time of the day or night I needed help. I call these my "2 A.M. friends."

As in our Aesop story today, you never know when you will need a friend. I have found that those who have friends are themselves friendly. They go out of their way to be a friend. In order to have friends, one must be a friend.

The skill of friendship-making is a skill that we need to teach our children. We as parents have only a short window of opportunity to teach the value of positive friendships to them. Each year we have less time for our influence on them. The music, dress, dance, and jewelry selections of the world seem to pull our children from our group. While there is still time, we need to steer our youngsters to choosing the right kind of friends.

*Father God, I thank You for the many wonderful*
*friends You have given me over the years. I*
*know how each one has been, and continues to*
*be, a support system for me. They cry with me,*
*laugh with me, pray with me, and hold me in*
*all of life's episodes. Be with the woman reader*
*today who lacks friends; may You reveal to her*
*ways of developing the kind of friends that will*
*stick closer than a brother or sister. Amen.*

*Notes*

1. Elon Foster, ed., *6000 Sermon Illustrations,* (Grand Rapids, MI: Baker Book House, 1992), adapted from p. 627.

2. Dr. R. Newton, *6000 Sermon Illustrations,* ed. Elon Foster (Grand Rapids, MI: Baker Book House, 1992), p. 309.

3. Lee Iacocca, *Straight Talk* (New York: Bantam Books, 1988), p. 27.

4. Bill Bright, *Four Spiritual Laws* (San Bernardino, CA: Campus Crusade for Christ, Inc., 1965), p. 10.

5. Lee Iacocca, *Straight Talk* (New York: Bantam Books, 1988), p. 270.

6. Harold L. Myra, *The Family Book of Christian Virtues,* edited by Stuart and Jill Briscoe (Colorado Springs, CO: Alive Communications, Inc., 1995), p. 252.

7. Jane Bluestein, comp., *Mentors, Masters and Mrs. MacGregor* (Deerfield Beach, FL: Health Communications, Inc., 1995), pp. 12-13.

8. Taken from *The Women's Devotional Bible.* Copyright © 1990 by The Zondervan Corporation. Used by permission of Zondervan Publishing House.

9. Books by Marilyn Willett Heavilin: *Roses in December; Becoming a Woman of Honor; When Your Dreams Die; December's Song; I'm Listening, Lord.*

10. Lee Iacocca, *Straight Talk* (New York: Bantam Books, 1988), p. 67.

11. June Hunt, *Seeing Yourself Through God's Eyes* (Grand Rapids, MI: Zondervan, 1989), p. 33.

12. Larry Crabb, *The Marriage Builder* (Grand Rapids, MI: Zondervan, 1982), p. 22.

13. Alan Loy McGinnis, *The Friendship Factor* (Minneapolis, MN: Augsburg, 1979), p. 23.

14. Robert H. Schuller, *Self-Esteem, The New Reformation* (Waco, TX: Word Publishing, 1982), pp. 17-18.

15. Bob Barnes, *Walking Together in Wisdom* (Eugene, OR: Harvest House Publishers, 2001), pp. 6-7,14,32.

16. Jerry and Barbara Cook, *Choosing to Love* (Ventura, CA: Regal Books, 1982) pp.78-80.

17. Erma Bombeck, further documentation unavailable.

18. Elon Foster, ed., *6000 Sermon Illustrations* (Grand Rapids, MI: Baker Book House, 1992), p. 353.

19. Ann Landers, *Press-Enterprise,* Riverside, CA, Saturday, May 11, 1996, p. B-10.

20. Adapted from Temple Bailey. This story first appeared in a pamphlet that Clifton's Cafeteria distributed to its customers in 1945.

# Harvest House Books by Bob & Emilie Barnes

## Bob & Emilie Barnes

*15-Minute Devotions
  for Couples*
*Be My Refuge, Lord*
*A Little Book of Manners
  for Boys*
*Minute Meditations
  for Couples*
*Simple Secrets Every Couple
  Should Know*

## Bob Barnes

*5-Minute Bible Workouts for Men*
*15 Minutes Alone
  with God for Men*
*Men Under Construction*
*What Makes a Man
  Feel Loved*

## Emilie Barnes

*The 15-Minute Organizer*
*15 Minutes Alone with God*
*15 Minutes of Peace
  with God*
*15 Minutes with God
  for Grandma*
*101 Ways to Clean Out the Clutter*
*500 Time-Saving Hints
  for Every Woman*
*Christmas Teas of Comfort and Joy*
*Cleaning Up the Clutter*
*Emilie's Creative
  Home Organizer*
*Everything I Know
  I Learned in My Garden*
*Everything I Know
  I Learned over Tea*

*Friendship Teas to Go*
*Garden Moment Getaways*
*Good Manners for Every Occasion*
*A Grandma Is a Gift from God*
*Heal My Heart, Lord*
*Home Warming*
*If Teacups Could Talk*
*I Need Your Strength, Lord*
*An Invitation to Tea*
*Journey through Cancer*
*Let's Have a Tea Party!*
*A Little Book of Manners*
*A Little Hero in the Making*
*A Little Princess in the Making*
*The Little Teacup that Talked*
*Meet Me Where I Am, Lord*
*Minute Meditations for Busy Moms*
*Minute Meditations for Healing
  and Hope*
*More Faith in My Day*
*More Hours in My Day*
*The Quick-Fix Home Organizer*
*Quiet Moments Alone with God*
*A Quiet Refuge*
*Safe in the Father's Hands*
*Simple Secrets to
  a Beautiful Home*
*A Tea to Comfort Your Soul*
*The Twelve Teas®
  of Friendship*
*The Twelve Teas® of Inspiration*
*Walk with Me Today, Lord*
*What Makes a Woman Feel Loved*
*Youniquely Woman*